cooking
curries

cooking
curries

Jane Lawson

THUNDER BAY
P·R·E·S·S

San Diego, California

contents

a world of flavor

For such a humble sounding word, *curry* refers to some of the world's most delicious and popular dishes. The British in India first coined the word itself, possibly derived from the Tamil word *kari*, meaning "spiced sauce." Today the term includes dishes that range from simple to sophisticated, complex to singularly bold, those that can be made in minutes or left for hours over a bed of coals, and includes the everyday food of peasants to the once-exclusive creations of the rich and royal.

Use of the word has expanded to include the curries of Southeast Asia alongside those of India, and this book features dishes from cuisines as varied as those of Kashmir, Goa, Bangladesh, Thailand, Malaysia, Sri Lanka, Laos, and Vietnam. Despite this diversity, all curries share a few essential elements: a curry paste, seasonings—which can vary from fresh herbs to pungent shrimp paste—and the main ingredient, such as meat, fish, legumes, or vegetables. From there, curries can go in many directions. They may be dry, oily, wet, thick, or thin. The cooking can involve frying, boiling, steaming, or slow, gentle braising. Adjectives such as sour, salty, hot, sweet, creamy, pungent, and fragrant may all be applied to a finished dish, more often than not in combination. In fact, if anything unites curries, it is their skill in blending various tastes, textures, and aromas to create superb dishes of great depth and balance.

The essential starting place is the curry paste. The paste will infuse the other ingredients with its flavor and fragrance, and its creation is a real part of the pleasure of making a curry. Traditionally, curry pastes are made by hand, the ingredients added one-by-one to a mortar for grinding or to the frying pan for roasting, with the cook observing, smelling, and adjusting as necessary. Buying prepared spice mixtures is convenient, but to experience the real thing, try preparing one from scratch.

Of course, the other thing that unites curries is rice. This staple of life is central to the cuisines of India and Southeast Asia, and curries support the rice— not the other way around. Once again, the trick is to seek balance, combining delicately perfumed rice with vegetable dishes, side dishes, and curries to match. This book contains some classic raitas, pickles, and breads to experiment with and many more wonderful curries that amply demonstrate the delight to be found in this age-old dish.

rich

Creamy, smooth curries are often the best place to start if new to curries. In fact, many of the world's favorite curries belong to this type—the most common examples include butter chicken, Thai musaman beef curry, Indian lamb kormas, and the many kofta or meatball recipes that are served on a bed of rich, creamy sauce. These curries have coconut milk, ground nuts, and yogurt or cream as their base, sometimes singly but often in combination.

Coconut is perhaps the most versatile of these products. It harmonizes flavors, subdues the potency of fiery chilies, and balances sour ingredients such as Thai apple eggplants, tart lime juice, and salty shrimp paste. The taste of the coconut itself is also important. Fresh coconut cream, in particular, enriches the curry with its own depth of flavor, so that dishes are complex and sumptuous—not merely creamy.

Canned coconut cream does not have the same qualities as fresh coconut but is much easier to obtain, so the recipes in this chapter call for the canned variety. In many of the recipes, it is recommended that you do not shake the can, as the thick cream on the top can be used to fry the paste, with just a little oil added. Simmering the coconut cream before adding the curry paste evaporates most of the water and ensures the curry paste is fried, not boiled, as the cream becomes quite oily.

Many of the dishes in this chapter come from tropical areas of India and Thailand, where coconut trees flourish. Every part of the tree is used, from thatching for houses to making lotions for the skin and hair from the oil. In India, coconut forms the base of golden, thick korma-style curries, perfected by the Moguls in the seventeenth century, as well as the yogurt-based dumpling dishes of Gujarat and the spicy seafood curries of coastal Goa. Thai uses of coconut are just as varied and delicious. Their spicy red curries, the sharp green curries, and the panaeng and musaman curries of the south all use coconut as their starting point.

In contrast to coconut, yogurt is more often used as a thickener and meat tenderizer than as a flavoring, producing wonderfully tender, slow-cooked curries of lamb and beef. It is also the key ingredient in soothing Indian raitas, for which many of us have been thankful.

thai beef and peanut curry

LIKE ALL THAI CURRIES, THE KEY TO THIS DISH IS BALANCE: IT HAS A SWEET, SPICY, AND SALTY PASTE COMBINED WITH THE RICH SMOOTHNESS OF PEANUTS AND COCONUT. CHOOSE A BEEF CUT THAT WILL BENEFIT FROM SLOW COOKING. TO ROAST THE PEANUTS YOURSELF, COOK IN A 350°F OVEN FOR 8–10 MINUTES OR UNTIL GOLDEN.

curry paste

dried long red chilies	8–10
red Asian shallots	6, chopped
garlic	6 cloves
ground coriander	1 teaspoon
ground cumin	1 tablespoon
ground white pepper	1 teaspoon
lemongrass	2 stems, white part only, sliced
galangal	1 tablespoon chopped
cilantro	6 roots
shrimp paste	2 teaspoons
roasted peanuts	2 tablespoons
peanut oil	1 tablespoon, optional
unsweetened coconut cream	14 fluid-ounce can
	(do not shake the can)
round or blade steak	2 pounds, 4 ounces, thinly sliced
unsweetened coconut milk	14 fluid-ounce can, or 1²/₃ cups
Kaffir lime leaves	4
crunchy peanut butter	¹/₃ cup
lime juice	3 tablespoons
fish sauce	2¹/₂ tablespoons
jaggery	2¹/₂ tablespoons shaved
	(or 2¹/₂ tablespoons brown sugar)
Thai basil leaves	optional, to serve
roasted peanuts	1 tablespoon chopped, optional, to serve

Soak the chilies in boiling water for 5 minutes or until soft. Remove the stem and seeds, then chop. Put the chilies and the remaining curry paste ingredients in a food processor or in a mortar with a pestle, and process or pound to a smooth paste. Add a little peanut oil if it is too thick.

Put the thick coconut cream from the top of the can in a saucepan, bring to a rapid simmer over medium heat, stirring occasionally, and cook for 5–10 minutes or until the mixture "splits" (the oil starts to separate). Add 6–8 tablespoons of the curry paste. Stirring, cook for an additional 5–10 minutes or until fragrant.

Add the beef, the remaining coconut cream, coconut milk, lime leaves, and peanut butter. Cook for 8 minutes or until the beef just starts to change color. Reduce the heat and simmer for 1 hour or until the beef is tender.

Stir in the lime juice, fish sauce, and jaggery, and transfer to a serving dish. Garnish with the basil and extra peanuts, if desired.

Remove the stem and seeds and chop the softened chilies.

Use a food processor to process the paste ingredients quickly.

pork curry with eggplant . . . . serves 4

PORK IS A FAVORITE MEAT ACROSS MUCH OF INDIA AND SOUTHEAST ASIA, BUT IS USED IN RELATIVELY FEW CURRIES. WHEN IT IS USED, IT IS OFTEN TEAMED WITH OTHER RICH FLAVORS, SUCH AS COCONUT. DON'T RUSH THIS DISH, AS THE SLOW, GENTLE COOKING ENSURES VERY TENDER MEAT.

curry paste

long red chilies	4, split lengthwise, seeded
galangal	1 thick slice, chopped
scallion	1, chopped
garlic	2 cloves, chopped
cilantro	2 roots, chopped
lemongrass	1 stem, white part only, thinly sliced
ground white pepper	1 teaspoon
shrimp paste	1/2 teaspoon
fish sauce	1 teaspoon
crunchy peanut butter	2 tablespoons

pork shoulder	1 pound 5 ounces
ginger	1 thick slice
jaggery	2 tablespoons shaved (or 2 tablespoons brown sugar)
fish sauce	1/3 cup
unsweetened coconut cream	14 fluid-ounce can (do not shake the can)
eggplant	1/2, cut into 3/4-inch cubes
bamboo shoots	1 cup canned, drained, sliced
Thai basil leaves	1 large handful, chopped

Put the split chilies in a shallow bowl. Pour enough hot water over to just cover. Let sit for 15 minutes, or until softened. Drain, reserving 1 tablespoon of the soaking liquid.

Except the peanut butter, combine the remaining curry paste ingredients, the chilies, and reserved soaking liquid in a food processor or in a mortar with a pestle. Process or pound to a smooth paste. Stir in the peanut butter.

Cut the pork into 1/2-inch-thick slices. Put in a saucepan and cover with water. Add the ginger, 1 tablespoon of the jaggery, and 1 tablespoon of the fish sauce. Bring to a boil over high heat, then reduce to a simmer and cook for 20–25 minutes or until the meat is tender. Remove from the heat and allow the meat to cool in the liquid stock. Strain, reserving 1 cup of the cooking liquid.

Put the thick coconut cream from the top of the can in a saucepan. Bring to a rapid simmer over medium heat, stir occasionally, and cook for 5–10 minutes or until the mixture "splits" (the oil starts to separate). Add the curry paste and the remaining jaggery and fish sauce, and bring to a boil. Reduce to a simmer and cook for about 3 minutes or until fragrant. Add the pork, eggplant, bamboo shoots, the reserved pork cooking liquid, and the remaining coconut cream. Increase the heat and bring to a boil again, then reduce to a simmer and cook for an additional 20–25 minutes or until the eggplant is tender and the sauce has thickened slightly. Serve garnished with the basil leaves.

Split the chilies, then scrape away the seeds with a knife.

Stir the peanut butter into the paste, mixing until smooth.

musaman vegetable curry . . . . serves 4–6

THIS CURRY IS A GOOD ONE TO TRY IF YOU ARE NEW TO CURRIES. IT IS SUMPTUOUSLY SPICED AND SEASONED WITHOUT BEING FIERY OR OVERLY RICH, AND HAS A LIGHTNESS OF FLAVOR NOT SEEN IN MANY MEAT CURRIES. SIMILARLY, THE SAUCE IS THICK, NEITHER TOO WET NOR DRY, AND PERFECT FOR SCOOPING UP WITH RICE OR BREAD.

musaman curry paste

oil	1 tablespoon
coriander seeds	1 teaspoon
cumin seeds	1 teaspoon
cloves	8
fennel seeds	1/2 teaspoon
cardamom seeds	4
red Asian shallots	6, chopped
garlic	3 cloves, chopped
lemongrass	1 teaspoon finely chopped, white part only
galangal	1 teaspoon finely chopped
dried long red chilies	4
ground nutmeg	1 teaspoon
ground white pepper	1 teaspoon

oil	1 tablespoon
pearl onions	5
baby new potatoes	8 (about 1 pound in total)
carrots	2, cut into 1 1/4-inch pieces
baby button mushrooms (champignons)	8 ounces canned, whole, drained
cinnamon stick	1
Kaffir lime leaf	1
bay leaf	1
unsweetened coconut cream	1 cup
lime juice	1 tablespoon
jaggery	3 teaspoons shaved (or 3 teaspoons brown sugar)
Thai basil leaves	1 tablespoon finely chopped, plus extra to serve
roasted peanuts	1 tablespoon crushed

Heat the oil in a frying pan over low heat. Add the coriander seeds, cumin seeds, cloves, fennel seeds, and cardamom seeds and cook for 1–2 minutes or until fragrant.

Combine the spices with the remaining curry paste ingredients in a food processor or in a mortar with a pestle. Process or pound to a smooth paste. Add a little water if it is too thick.

Heat the oil in a large saucepan and add the curry paste. Stirring, cook over medium heat for 2 minutes or until fragrant. Add the vegetables, cinnamon stick, lime leaf, bay leaf, and enough water to cover (about 2 cups). Bring to a boil. Reduce the heat and simmer covered, stirring frequently, for 30–35 minutes or until the vegetables are cooked.

Stir in the coconut cream and cook uncovered for 4 minutes, stirring frequently, until thickened slightly. Stir in the lime juice, jaggery, and chopped basil. Add a little water if the sauce is too dry. Garnish with the peanuts and basil leaves.

thai red duck curry with pineapple .... serves 4–6

THE ART OF THAI CURRIES——AND THE REASON WHY WE KEEP COMING BACK TO THEM——IS THE WAY THEY COMBINE DIFFERENT FLAVORS AND TEXTURES IN THE ONE DISH TO CREATE A HARMONIOUS WHOLE. THIS DISH IS A PERFECT EXAMPLE OF THAT SKILL, BLENDING SWEET, SAVORY, AND SPICY INGREDIENTS WITH RICH COCONUT MILK.

red curry paste

dried long red chilies	15
white peppercorns	1 tablespoon
coriander seeds	2 teaspoons
cumin seeds	1 teaspoon
shrimp paste	2 teaspoons
red Asian shallots	5, chopped
garlic	10 cloves, chopped
lemongrass	2 stems, white part only, thinly sliced
galangal	1 tablespoon chopped
cilantro	2 tablespoons chopped root
Kaffir lime zest	1 teaspoon finely grated
peanut oil	1 tablespoon
scallions	8, sliced diagonally into 1¼-inch lengths
garlic	2 cloves, crushed
Chinese barbecued duck	1, chopped into large pieces (see note)
unsweetened coconut milk	14 fluid-ounce can, or 1⅔ cups
pineapple pieces in syrup	16-ounce can, drained
Kaffir lime leaves	3
cilantro	3 tablespoons chopped leaves
mint	2 tablespoons chopped

Soak the chilies in boiling water for 5 minutes or until soft. Remove the stem and seeds, then chop. Dry-fry the peppercorns, coriander seeds, cumin seeds, and shrimp paste wrapped in foil in a frying pan over medium–high heat for 2–3 minutes, or until fragrant. Allow to cool. Using a mortar with a pestle or a spice grinder, crush or grind the peppercorns, coriander, and cumin to a powder.

Combine the chopped chilies, shrimp paste, and ground spices with the remaining curry paste ingredients in a food processor or in a mortar with a pestle. Process or pound to a smooth paste.

Heat a wok until very hot. Add the oil and swirl to coat the side. Add the scallion, garlic, and 2–4 tablespoons of the red curry paste. Stir-fry for 1 minute or until fragrant.

Add the roast duck pieces, coconut milk, drained pineapple pieces, lime leaves, and half the cilantro and mint. Bring to a boil, then reduce the heat and simmer for 10 minutes or until the duck is heated through and the sauce thickens slightly. Stir in the remaining cilantro and mint before serving.

Note: Chinese barbecued ducks can be purchased from Chinese restaurants.

fish and peanut curry .... serves 6

ONE OF THE STAR INGREDIENTS IN THIS DISH IS CRISP FRIED ONIONS, WHICH CAN BE BOUGHT FROM ASIAN FOOD STORES OR EASILY PREPARED AT HOME (SEE NOTE BELOW). AS WELL, USE DRIED SPICES AND SOUR TAMARIND TO NICELY BALANCE THE CREAMY, NUTTY FLAVORS OF THIS DISH.

sesame seeds	1/3 cup
cayenne pepper	1/2 teaspoon
ground turmeric	1/4 teaspoon
dried coconut	1 tablespoon
ground coriander	2 teaspoons
ground cumin	1/2 teaspoon
crisp fried onions	1/2 cup
ginger	2-inch piece, chopped
garlic	2 cloves, chopped
tamarind puree	3 tablespoons
crunchy peanut butter	1 tablespoon
roasted peanuts	1 tablespoon
curry leaves	8, plus extra to serve
skinless, firm white fish fillets	2 pounds 4 ounces, cut into 3/4-inch cubes
lemon juice	1 tablespoon

In a heavy-based frying pan over medium heat, stir the sesame seeds until golden. Add the cayenne pepper, turmeric, coconut, ground coriander, and cumin and stir for 1 minute, or until aromatic. Set aside to cool.

Combine the fried onions, ginger, garlic, tamarind, peanut butter, roasted peanuts, sesame spice mix, 1 teaspoon salt, and 2 cups hot water in a food processor. Process until the mixture reaches a smooth, thick consistency.

Over medium heat, bring the sauce and curry leaves to a simmer in a heavy-based frying pan. Cover, reduce to low heat, and simmer for 15 minutes, then add the fish in a single layer. Simmer covered for an additional 5 minutes or until the fish is just cooked through. Gently stir in the lemon juice, and season well to taste. Garnish with the extra curry leaves and serve.

Note: To make crisp fried onions at home, very thinly slice 1 onion, then dry on paper towels for 10 minutes. Fill a deep, heavy-based saucepan one-third full of oil and heat to 315°F or until a cube of bread dropped into the oil browns in 30 seconds. Fry the onions for up to 1 minute or until they are crisp and golden. Drain well, then cool and store in an airtight container for up to two weeks. Use as a garnish and flavor enhancer for curries, rice, and noodle dishes.

Stir the sesame seeds over medium heat until lightly golden.

Add the spices to the frying pan and stir until aromatic.

Add the fish in a single layer to the simmering sauce.

three ways with rice

IT IS IMPOSSIBLE TO OVERESTIMATE THE IMPORTANCE OF RICE FOR THE PEOPLES OF SOUTHEAST ASIA AND INDIA. INDEED, CURRIES SUPPORT THE RICE, NOT THE OTHER WAY AROUND. RICE IS COMBINED WITH INGREDIENTS RANGING FROM THE MOST HUMBLE TO THE MOST LUXURIOUS. SAFFRON, THE WORLD'S MOST EXPENSIVE SPICE, IS USED TO FLAVOR INDIAN AND PERSIAN RICE DISHES, SUCH AS PILAF AND BIRYANI. OTHER STAPLES SUCH AS LENTILS AND COCONUT ARE ALSO COMMON, AND DELICIOUS, ADDITIONS TO RICE.

saffron rice

Wash 2 cups basmati rice, cover with cold water, and soak for 30 minutes. Then drain. Melt 2 tablespoons butter in a frying pan over medium heat, then add 3 bay leaves and the drained rice. Stirring, cook for 6 minutes or until all the moisture has evaporated. Meanwhile, soak 1/4 teaspoon saffron threads in 2 tablespoons hot water for a few minutes, then add to the rice with 2 cups boiling vegetable stock, 1 1/2 cups boiling water, and season with salt. Bring to a boil, then reduce the heat and cook covered for 12–15 minutes or until all the water has absorbed and the rice is cooked. Serves 6.

seasoned rice and lentils

Wash 1 1/2 cups basmati rice and 1 2/3 cups split mung beans (mung lentils), then drain and set aside. Heat 2 tablespoons oil in a frying pan, add 1 sliced onion, 3 bay leaves, 1 teaspoon cumin seeds, 2 pieces cassia bark, 1 tablespoon cardamom seeds, 6 cloves, and 1/4 teaspoon black peppercorns. Cook over low heat for 5 minutes or until the onion is softened and the spices are fragrant. Add the rice and lentils and cook, stirring, for 2 minutes. Pour in 5 cups water and season with salt. Bring to a boil, then reduce the heat and cook covered over low heat for 15 minutes. Stir gently to avoid breaking the grains and cook uncovered over low heat for 3 minutes or until all the moisture evaporates. Discard the whole spices when the dish is cooked. Serves 6.

coconut rice

Rinse 2 cups long-grained rice and cover with 4 cups water. Set aside for 30 minutes, then drain. Bring 3 cups water to a boil. Add the rice, 1 fresh screw-pine (pandanus) leaf tied in a knot, and season with salt. Reduce the heat and cook covered for 12 minutes or until the rice is just cooked. Remove from the heat and add 3/4 cup unsweetened coconut cream. Stir gently to avoid breaking the grains. Cover and set aside for 10 minutes or until the rice absorbs the coconut cream in the residual heat. Discard the screw-pine leaf before serving. Serves 6.

saffron rice

lamb shank and yogurt curry

THIS IS NOT A CURRY TO MAKE AT THE LAST MINUTE, BUT THE SLOW COOKING PRODUCES WONDERFULLY TENDER MEAT, WHILE ALSO ALLOWING FOR THE SUBTLE AROMAS AND FLAVORS OF THE SPICES TO EMERGE AND BLEND. LAMB SHANK IS IDEAL FOR THIS, AND USING YOGURT THICKENS THE SAUCE AND ROUNDS OFF THE DISH.

coriander seeds	3 tablespoons
cumin seeds	2 teaspoons
cloves	1 teaspoon
black peppercorns	1 teaspoon
cayenne pepper	1/2 teaspoon
ground turmeric	1 teaspoon
ginger	2 tablespoons chopped
garlic	6 cloves, chopped
onion	1 small, chopped
ghee or oil	2 tablespoons
lamb shanks	6
cinnamon sticks	3
bay leaves	2
plain yogurt	1 1/2 cups
chicken stock	2 1/2 cups

Preheat the oven to 315°F.

Dry-fry the coriander seeds, cumin seeds, cloves, peppercorns, cayenne pepper, and ground turmeric in a frying pan over medium-high heat for 2–3 minutes or until fragrant. Allow to cool. Using a mortar with a pestle or a spice grinder, crush or grind to a powder.

Combine the ground spices with the ginger, garlic, onion, and 3 tablespoons water in a food processor or in a mortar with a pestle, and process or pound to a smooth paste.

In a large, heavy-based frying pan, heat the ghee or oil over medium-high heat and brown the shanks in batches. Set aside. Reduce the heat to low. Add the ginger spice paste to the frying pan and cook for 5–8 minutes. Add the cinnamon stick and bay leaves to the pan. Add the yogurt a spoonful at a time, stirring well so it incorporates smoothly. Add the stock and stir well to combine.

In a large, heavy-based ovenproof dish, place the shanks in a single layer, then pour the yogurt sauce over the top of the shanks. Turn the shanks so the sauce coats them, and cover with a lid or foil. Bake in the oven for about 3 hours or until the lamb falls from the bone, turning the shanks halfway through cooking. When removing them from the oven, skim and discard any oil that surfaces.

Remove the shanks from the sauce and place onto a serving platter. Season the sauce well, stirring to mix, before spooning over the shanks.

thai red beef curry
with thai eggplants .... serves 4

BASIC RED CURRIES VARY GREATLY, BUT ALL ARE DISTINGUISHED BY THE DARK SHADE OF THE SAUCE. THE COLOR, OF COURSE, COMES FROM A GOOD DOSE OF DRIED LONG RED CHILIES IN THE PASTE. MOST RED CURRIES ARE WET (NOT DRY), AND FRAGRANT WITH FRESH KAFFIR LIME AND THAI BASIL.

round or topside steak	1 pound 2 ounces
unsweetened coconut cream	9 fluid ounces canned
	(do not shake the can)
red curry paste	2 tablespoons, store-bought or
	see recipe on page 18
fish sauce	2 tablespoons
jaggery	1 tablespoon shaved
	(or 1 tablespoon brown sugar)
Kaffir lime leaves	5, halved
unsweetened coconut milk	2 cups
Thai apple eggplants	8, halved
Thai basil leaves	1 small handful, finely shredded

Cut the meat into 2-inch pieces, then cut across the grain at a 45-degree angle into ¼-inch-thick slices.

Put the thick coconut cream from the top of the can in a saucepan, and bring to a rapid simmer over medium heat. Stirring occasionally, cook for 5–10 minutes or until the mixture "splits" (the oil starts to separate). Add the red curry paste and simmer for 5 minutes or until fragrant, stirring to prevent it from sticking to the bottom of the pan.

Stirring still, add the beef and cook for 3–5 minutes or until it changes color. Add the fish sauce, jaggery, lime leaves, coconut milk, and remaining coconut cream and simmer for 1 hour or until the meat is tender and the sauce is slightly thickened.

Add the eggplant and cook for 10 minutes or until tender. If the sauce is too thick, add a little water. Stir in the basil leaves and serve.

This tropical Asian fruit comes in an array of shapes, sizes, and colors that would surprise most people. In Thailand alone, popular eggplant varieties include long, skinny, pale green ones—similar to purple Japanese baby eggplants, but milder—as well as Thai apple eggplants (confusingly, the size of golf balls), which are full of seeds and can be quite bitter. Both have specific uses in Thai cooking: the former in green curries, and the latter in salads, curries, and relishes. Other varieties are the sour-tasting fuzzy eggplants and pea eggplants. This last type grows in clusters and tastes bitter, but is valued precisely for that quality. They are sometimes available pickled in jars.

rich chicken koftas

KOFTA MIGHT CONTAIN MEAT, FISH, OR VEGETABLES, ALL WELL-COMBINED MIXTURES, WITH ADDED HERBS AND SPICES. ACCOMPANYING SAUCES ARE EQUALLY APPEALING—IN THIS DISH, THE SAUCE IS RICH WITH COCONUT, YOGURT, CREAM, AND ALMONDS, BALANCED BY THE SPICY, PEPPERY NOTES OF GARAM MASALA AND TURMERIC.

koftas

oil	2 tablespoons
onion	1, finely chopped
garlic	1 clove, crushed
ginger	1 teaspoon finely chopped
ground cumin	1 teaspoon
garam masala	1 teaspoon
ground turmeric	1/2 teaspoon
boneless, skinless chicken thighs	1 pound 7 ounces, trimmed
cilantro	2 tablespoons chopped leaves
onion	1, roughly chopped
ghee or oil	1 tablespoon
garlic	2 cloves, crushed
garam masala	2 teaspoons
ground turmeric	1/2 teaspoon
unsweetened coconut milk	2/3 cup
plain yogurt	1/3 cup
whipping cream	1/2 cup
ground almonds	1/3 cup
cilantro	2 tablespoons chopped leaves

To make the koftas, heat half the oil in a frying pan. Add the onion, garlic, ginger, cumin, garam masala, and turmeric. Stirring, cook for 4–6 minutes or until the onion is tender and the spices are fragrant. Allow to cool.

In batches, process the chicken in a food processor until just chopped. Do not overprocess the mixture.

Put the chicken, onion mixture, cilantro, and 1/2 teaspoon salt in a bowl and mix together well. Using wetted hands, measure 1 tablespoon of the mixture and shape into a ball. Repeat with the remaining mixture. Heat the remaining oil in a heavy-based frying pan, add the koftas in batches, and cook for 4–5 minutes or until well browned all over. Remove from the pan and cover.

Put the second onion in a food processor and process until smooth. Heat the ghee or oil in a frying pan. Add the onion and garlic and cook, stirring, for 5 minutes or until the onion juices evaporate and the mixture starts to thicken. Add the garam masala and turmeric and cook for 2 minutes. Add the coconut milk, yogurt, cream, and ground almonds. Gently bring almost to a boil, then reduce the heat to medium and add the koftas. Stirring occasionally, cook for 15 minutes or until the koftas are cooked through. Stir in the cilantro and serve.

Combine the chicken, onion mixture, cilantro, and salt.

Use wetted hands to shape the chicken mixture into balls.

Fry the chicken koftas in batches and remove from the pan.

lamb korma..serves 4

A FAMILIAR STAPLE OF INDIAN RESTAURANTS AROUND THE WORLD, KORMA IS MORE THAN A DISH—IT IS A COOKING STYLE. PUT SIMPLY, IT CONSISTS OF MARINATED MEAT OR VEGETABLES THAT ARE COOKED WITH GHEE OR OIL, THEN BRAISED WITH WATER OR STOCK, YOGURT, OR CREAM (OR SOMETIMES ALL OF THESE).

lamb leg meat	2 pound 4 ounces
onion	1, chopped, plus 1 sliced
ginger	2 teaspoons grated
garlic	4 cloves
ground coriander	2 teaspoons
ground cumin	2 teaspoons
cardamom seeds	1 teaspoon
cloves	1/4 teaspoon
ground cinnamon	1/4 teaspoon
long green chilies	3, seeded, chopped
ghee or oil	2 tablespoons
tomato paste	2 1/2 tablespoons
plain yogurt	1/2 cup
unsweetened coconut cream	1/2 cup
ground almonds	1/2 cup
toasted slivered almonds	to serve

Trim any excess fat or sinew from the lamb. Cut into 1¼-inch cubes and put in a large bowl.

Combine the chopped onion, ginger, garlic, coriander, cumin, cardamom seeds, cloves, cinnamon, chilies, and 1/2 teaspoon salt in a food processor or in a mortar with a pestle. Process or pound to a smooth paste. Add the spice paste to the lamb and mix well to coat. Leave to marinate for 1 hour.

Heat the ghee or oil in a large saucepan, add the sliced onion and cook, stirring, over low heat for 7 minutes or until the onion is soft. Increase the heat to medium-high and add the lamb mixture. Stirring constantly, cook for 8–10 minutes or until the lamb changes color.

Stir in the tomato paste, yogurt, coconut cream, and ground almonds. Reduce the heat and simmer covered, stirring occasionally, for about 1 hour or until the meat is very tender. Add a little water if the mixture becomes too dry. Season well with salt and pepper, and serve garnished with the slivered almonds.

Add the spice paste to the lamb to marinate.

Add the lamb mixture to the pan and cook until it changes color.

scallop and shrimp chu chee................serves 4

CHU CHEE CURRY PASTE IS THE TRADITIONAL THAI FLAVOR BASE FOR SEAFOOD. IT IS SIMILAR TO A RED CURRY PASTE IN THAT DRIED RED CHILIES DOMINATE, BUT THE PROPORTION OF AROMATICS SUCH AS GALANGAL, LEMONGRASS, KAFFIR LIME LEAVES, AND CILANTRO ARE GREATER.

chu chee curry paste

dried long red chilies	10
shrimp paste	1 tablespoon
coriander seeds	1 teaspoon
white peppercorns	1 tablespoon
Kaffir lime leaves	10, finely shredded
red Asian shallots	10, chopped
Kaffir lime zest	2 teaspoons finely grated
cilantro	1 tablespoon chopped stem and root
lemongrass	1 stem, white part only, finely chopped
galangal	3 tablespoons chopped
krachai	1 tablespoon chopped, optional (see note)
garlic	6 cloves, crushed
unsweetened coconut cream	18 1/2 fluid ounces canned (do not shake the cans)
scallops	1 pound 2 ounces, with roe removed
raw jumbo shrimp	1 pound 2 ounces, peeled, deveined, tails intact
fish sauce	2–3 tablespoons
jaggery	2–3 tablespoons shaved (or 2–3 tablespoons brown sugar)
Kaffir lime leaves	8, finely shredded
red chilies	2, thinly sliced
Thai basil leaves	1 large handful

Soak the chilies in boiling water for 5 minutes or until soft. Remove the stem and seeds, then chop. Wrap the shrimp paste in foil and dry-fry it with the coriander seeds and peppercorns in a frying pan over medium-high heat for 2–3 minutes or until fragrant. Allow to cool. Using a mortar with a pestle or a spice grinder, crush or grind the coriander and peppercorns to a powder.

Combine the chopped chilies, shrimp paste, and ground coriander and peppercorns with the remaining curry paste ingredients in a food processor or in a mortar with a pestle. Process or pound to a smooth paste.

Put the thick coconut cream from the top of the cans in a saucepan, bring to a rapid simmer over medium heat, stirring occasionally, and cook for 5–10 minutes or until the mixture "splits" (the oil starts to separate). Stir in 3 tablespoons of the curry paste, then reduce the heat and simmer for 10 minutes or until fragrant.

Stir in the remaining coconut cream, scallops, and shrimp. Cook for 5 minutes or until tender. Add the fish sauce, jaggery, lime leaves, and chilies and cook for 1 minute. Stir in half the basil and garnish with the remaining leaves.

Note: Krachai (bottled lesser galangal) is available from Asian food stores. It can be omitted from the paste if unavailable.

the perfect curry paste

Commercially produced curry pastes certainly have their place, but nothing will ever compete with a fresh, homemade batch—the benefits far outweighing the effort. Not only will your curry have better flavor, but a certain amount of joy is involved in selecting, sniffing, and touching fresh, exotic ingredients, then taking the time and care to finely grind them, releasing fresh and spicy aromas into your home. It is the aromas and flavors generated by the release of natural oils during the grinding process that makes a made-from-scratch curry unique and irresistible. You can also keep excess curry paste in an airtight container in the refrigerator for one week, or in the freezer for up to two months.

If you follow the guidelines below in conjunction with individual curry recipes, you will achieve great results every time. First, any fresh produce required should be just that—fresh, as well as firm, crisp, unblemished, and aromatic. Shriveled leafy herbs and chilies, dried garlic, ginger, and lemongrass, or soft onions will result in an inferior product. To obtain the maximum flavor and aroma from your curry pastes, put fresh ingredients into the hollow of a mortar, then pound and grind with a pestle until the mixture becomes pulpy, then as smooth as possible. This can take some time but it is worth it, not only flavorwise but for ensuring your curry has a consistent texture.

Buy spices in small quantities and use them up quickly, as they deteriorate when exposed to air. Fresh whole spices contain more essential oils—and therefore flavor—than preground spices or those that have been sitting in the cupboard for some time. To release the oils and make the spices more brittle for grinding, dry-fry the spices in a frying pan over medium-high heat for 2–3 minutes or until fragrant. To grind the spices, allow them to cool, then tip into a mortar and pound with a pestle until finely ground. The grinding releases the flavors and aromas and allows them to travel more evenly through the curry.

butter chicken

FOR MANY WESTERNERS, THIS FAMOUS DISH IS THEIR FIRST EXPERIENCE OF INDIAN FOOD. BASED ON TANDOORI CHICKEN, BUT WITHOUT THE TANDOOR, IT IS A RICH BLEND OF AROMATIC SPICES, BUTTER OR GHEE, YOGURT, AND TOMATO PASTE. WHEN DONE PROPERLY, IT IS SUMPTUOUS AND VELVETY, NOT MERELY CREAMY.

peanut oil	2 tablespoons
boneless, skinless chicken thighs	2 pounds 4 ounces, quartered
butter or ghee	1/3 cup
garam masala	3 teaspoons
sweet paprika	2 teaspoons
ground coriander	1 tablespoon
ginger	1 tablespoon finely chopped
ground cumin	3 teaspoons
garlic	2 cloves, crushed
chili powder	1/4 teaspoon
cinnamon stick	1
cardamom pods	5, bruised
tomato paste	2 1/2 tablespoons
sugar	1 tablespoon
plain yogurt	1/3 cup
whipping cream	3/4 cup
lemon juice	1 tablespoon

Heat a frying pan or wok until very hot, then add 1 tablespoon of the oil and swirl to coat. Add half the chicken and stir-fry for 4 minutes or until browned. Remove from the pan. Add extra oil, as needed, and cook the remaining chicken, then remove.

Reduce the heat, add the butter or ghee to the pan and melt. Add the garam masala, sweet paprika, coriander, ginger, cumin, garlic, chili powder, cinnamon stick, and cardamom pods. Stir-fry for 1 minute or until fragrant. Return the chicken to the pan and coat it well in the spices.

Add the tomato paste and sugar to the pan and simmer, stirring, for 15 minutes or until the chicken is tender and the sauce thickens. Add the yogurt, cream, and lemon juice and simmer for 5 minutes or until the sauce has thickened slightly.

Stir-fry the spices in a frying pan or wok until fragrant.

Coat the chicken well in the spice mixture.

Stir in the tomato paste and sugar and simmer.

musaman beef curry . . . . serves 4

THIS RICH, CREAMY CURRY IS A CLASSIC AMONG THAI CURRIES. ITS ORIGINS ARE UNCLEAR BUT TODAY IT IS MAINLY ASSOCIATED WITH THE SOUTHERN, MUSLIM AREAS OF THAILAND. COMPLEX WITH SWEET AND SOUR SPICES, IT IS UNUSUAL IN THAT IT ALSO INCORPORATES A STARCHY INGREDIENT SUCH AS POTATOES.

tamarind pulp	1 tablespoon
oil	2 tablespoons
lean stewing beef	1 pound 10 ounces, cubed
unsweetened coconut milk	2 cups
cardamom pods	4, bruised
unsweetened coconut cream	17 fluid ounces, canned (do not shake the cans)
musaman curry paste	2–3 tablespoons, store-bought or see recipe on page 17
pearl onions	8
baby potatoes	8, cut in half if too large
fish sauce	2 tablespoons
jaggery	2 tablespoons shaved (or 2 tablespoons brown sugar)
roasted ground peanuts	1/2 cup unsalted
cilantro	leaves, to serve, optional

Put the tamarind pulp and 1/2 cup boiling water in a bowl and set aside to cool. When cool, mash the pulp to dissolve in the water, then strain and reserve the liquid. Discard the pulp.

Heat the oil in a wok or a large saucepan and cook the beef in batches over high heat for 5 minutes or until browned. Reduce the heat and add the coconut milk and cardamom. Simmer for 1 hour or until the beef is tender. Remove the beef, strain, and reserve the beef and cooking liquid.

Put the thick coconut cream from the top of the cans in a saucepan, bring to a rapid simmer over medium heat, stirring occasionally, and cook for 5–10 minutes or until the mixture "splits" (the oil starts to separate). Add the curry paste and cook for 5 minutes or until aromatic.

Combine the onions, potatoes, fish sauce, jaggery, peanuts, beef, reserved cooking liquid, and tamarind liquid. Simmer for 25–30 minutes. Garnish with cilantro leaves.

Pour boiling water onto the tamarind pulp to soften it.

Mash the pulp together with the water until as smooth as possible.

Strain the mashed pulp to obtain the tamarind liquid.

thai yellow vegetable curry .... serves 6

YELLOW CURRIES ARE FROM THAILAND'S SOUTHERN AREAS AND ARE CHARACTERIZED BY THEIR USE OF SPICES SUCH AS CORIANDER, CUMIN, AND TURMERIC IN THE PASTE—THE TURMERIC PROVIDING THE LOVELY GOLDEN COLORING. THEY ARE USUALLY OF MEDIUM STRENGTH, WET RATHER THAN DRY, AND DELICATELY SPICED.

yellow curry paste

green chilies	8
red Asian shallots	5, chopped
garlic	2 cloves, crushed
cilantro	1 tablespoon finely chopped stem and root
lemongrass	1 stem, white part only, finely chopped
galangal	2 tablespoons finely chopped
ground coriander	1 teaspoon
ground cumin	1 teaspoon
ground turmeric	1/2 teaspoon
black peppercorns	1/2 teaspoon
lime juice	1 tablespoon
oil	3 tablespoons
onion	1, finely chopped
all-purpose potatoes	1 large, diced
zucchini	2, diced
red bell pepper	1/2, diced
green beans	20, trimmed, halved
bamboo shoots	1/4 cup canned, drained, sliced
vegetable stock	1 cup
unsweetened coconut cream	14 fluid-ounce can, or 1 2/3 cups
Thai basil leaves	to serve

Combine all the curry paste ingredients in a food processor or in a mortar with a pestle. Process or pound to a smooth paste.

Heat the oil in a large saucepan, add the onion, and cook over medium heat for 4–5 minutes or until softened and just turning golden. Add 2 tablespoons of the curry paste and cook, stirring, for 2 minutes or until fragrant.

Add all the vegetables and cook over high heat for 2 minutes, stirring. Pour in the vegetable stock, reduce the heat to medium, and cook covered for 15–20 minutes or until the vegetables are tender. Cook uncovered over high heat for 5–10 minutes or until the sauce has reduced slightly.

Stir in the coconut cream and season with salt to taste. Bring to a boil, stirring frequently. Then reduce the heat and simmer for 5 minutes. Garnish with the basil leaves.

earthy

The pleasure of many curries begins with the aroma that is released at the start of cooking, as dried spices roast and crackle in the wok or pan. This is especially true of the earthy curries, as they are called here. Spices such as cumin, fennel, coriander seeds, turmeric, and curry leaves all bring a warm, rounded, toasty aroma and flavor to curries. For these curries, aroma is of equal importance to flavor and texture.

Taking the time to grind and roast your own spices may seem like a luxury these days but it is one of the best and most enjoyable ways to learn about the different qualities of the spices that go into a curry. Coriander seeds, for example, have a sweet, heady aroma, suggestive of pine and pepper, while warm and bitter cumin is immediately distinctive. Fennel seeds have a subtle anise aroma and warm, sweet, intense flavor that mellows on roasting. Different yet, potent cloves with their sharp and woody flavors contribute to many curry powders. Hidden within the unassuming dull brown skin of the versatile, pungent turmeric root is a vibrantly colored golden interior that, as a ground powder, is used in countless curries to balance and enhance the other flavors.

Many of these spices have been known for millennia—coriander is mentioned in ancient Sanskrit texts, and turmeric was included in an Assyrian manuscript dating back to 600 BC. The longevity of these spices is reflected in some of the recipes in this chapter. Both aromatic and slow-cooking rogan josh, and the equally luxurious lamb dhansak from India have their origins in Persia, whose traditional cooking is renowned for its subtle and sophisticated use of spices. Also in this chapter is beef rendang, eaten throughout Indonesia and Malaysia. A classic of one-pot cooking, the meat is tender and the flavor welcoming. In a number of dishes from Sri Lanka, curry powders that typically feature cardamom, cloves, cumin seeds, coriander, and cinnamon are characterized by a dark, roasted flavor and aroma. Overall, the curries in this chapter share a depth of sensuous flavor and aroma that is not always anticipated—which makes cooking and eating them all the more enjoyable.

chicken and thai apple eggplant curry . . . . serves 4

THIS SAVORY CURRY HAS LOTS OF FLAVOR AND IS WELL BALANCED—NOT TOO HOT, SWEET, OR SOUR. THAI APPLE EGGPLANTS CAN BE A BIT OF AN ACQUIRED TASTE. WHEN FRESH, THEY ARE CRISP AND CLEAN AND ALMOST SWEET TASTING, BUT CAN BECOME QUITE BITTER WHEN OLD.

curry paste

shrimp paste	1 teaspoon
white peppercorns	1 teaspoon
dried shrimp	2 tablespoons
cilantro	2 tablespoons chopped root
lemongrass	3 stems, white part only, thinly sliced
garlic	3 cloves
ginger	1 tablespoon finely chopped
red chili	1, chopped
Kaffir lime leaves	4
fish sauce	3 tablespoons
lime juice	3 tablespoons
ground turmeric	1 teaspoon

boneless, skinless chicken thighs	1 pound 2 ounces
Thai apple eggplants	6–7
unsweetened coconut cream	14 fluid-ounce can (do not shake the can)
jaggery	2 tablespoons shaved (or 2 tablespoons brown sugar)
red bell pepper	1, sliced
water chestnuts	8-ounce can sliced, drained
cilantro	1 tablespoon chopped leaves
Thai basil leaves	1 tablespoon chopped

Wrap the shrimp paste in foil and dry-fry it with the peppercorns and dried shrimp in a frying pan over medium-high heat for 2–3 minutes or until fragrant. Allow to cool. Using a mortar with a pestle or a spice grinder, crush or grind the peppercorns to a powder. Process the dried shrimp in a small food processor until it becomes very finely shredded—forming a "floss."

Combine the crushed peppercorns, shredded dried shrimp, and the shrimp paste with the remaining curry paste ingredients in a food processor or in a mortar with a pestle. Process or pound to a smooth paste.

Cut the chicken into 1-inch cubes. Cut the eggplants into pieces of a similar size.

Put the thick coconut cream from the top of the can in a saucepan. Bring to a rapid simmer over medium heat, and stirring occasionally, cook for 5–10 minutes or until the mixture "splits" (the oil starts to separate). Add the curry paste and stir for 5–6 minutes or until fragrant, then add the jaggery and stir until dissolved.

Add the chicken, eggplant, bell pepper, water chestnuts, and half the remaining coconut cream. Bring to a boil, cover, and reduce to a simmer. Cook for 15 minutes or until the chicken is cooked and the eggplant is soft. Stir in the remaining coconut cream, the cilantro, and basil.

Note: Thai apple eggplants are available from Asian food stores over summer and into early fall.

Finely grind the peppercorns in a mortar or use a spice grinder.

Cut the eggplants into pieces similar in size to the chicken.

sri lankan pepper beef curry..serves 6

SRI LANKA BOASTS A CUISINE THAT HAS BEEN INFLUENCED BY THE INDIANS, MALAYS, PORTUGUESE, DUTCH, AND BRITISH. ITS CURRIES ARE MOSTLY COCONUT-BASED AND STRONG WITH SPICES. MANY, SUCH AS THIS ONE, ARE COOKED FOR HOURS, UNTIL THE THICK, FLAVORSOME SAUCE CLINGS TO THE BY-NOW TENDER MAIN INGREDIENT.

coriander seeds	1 tablespoon
cumin seeds	2 teaspoons
fennel seeds	1 teaspoon
black peppercorns	1 tablespoon
oil	3 tablespoons
beef chuck	2 pounds 4 ounces, diced
onions	2, finely diced
garlic	4 cloves, crushed
ginger	3 teaspoons finely grated
red chili	1, seeded, finely chopped
curry leaves	8
lemongrass	1 stem, white part only, finely chopped
lemon juice	2 tablespoons
unsweetened coconut milk	1 cup
beef stock	1 cup

Dry-fry the coriander seeds, cumin seeds, fennel seeds, and black peppercorns in a frying pan over medium-high heat for 2–3 minutes or until fragrant. Allow to cool. Using a mortar with a pestle or a spice grinder, crush or grind to a powder.

In a heavy-based saucepan, heat the oil over high heat, brown the beef in batches, and set aside. Reduce the heat to medium, add the onion, garlic, ginger, chili, curry leaves, and lemongrass. Cook for 5–6 minutes or until softened. Add the ground spices and cook for 3 minutes.

Put the beef back into the pan and stir well to coat with the spices. Add the lemon juice, coconut milk, and beef stock. Bring to a boil. Reduce the heat to low, cover, and cook for 2½ hours or until the beef is very tender and the sauce reduces. While cooking, skim and discard any oil that surfaces.

Stir the spices constantly to release the aroma.

Brown the beef in batches to ensure you don't crowd the pan.

Cook the onion and spices until the onion softens.

fish in yogurt curry .... serves 4

THE CREAMY TEXTURE OF THIS DISH BELIES THE DEPTH OF FLAVOR IT HAS FROM THE CUMIN, CORIANDER, AND TURMERIC. THICK YOGURT IS AN EXCELLENT WAY TO PROTECT THE FISH DURING COOKING AND ALSO ABSORBS SOME OF THE STING FROM THE CHILIES. FOR BEST RESULTS USE A THICK, SET YOGURT.

skinless, firm white fish fillets	2 pounds 4 ounces
oil	3 tablespoons
onion	1, chopped
ginger	2 tablespoons finely chopped
garlic	6 cloves, crushed
ground cumin	1 teaspoon
ground coriander	2 teaspoons
ground turmeric	1/4 teaspoon
garam masala	1 teaspoon
Greek-style yogurt	3/4 cup (or plain yogurt drained in cheesecloth)
long green chilies	4, seeded, finely chopped
cilantro	leaves, to serve

Cut each fish fillet into four pieces and thoroughly pat them dry. Heat the oil in a heavy-based frying pan over low heat and fry the onion until softened and lightly browned. Add the ginger, garlic, and spices and stir for 2 minutes. Add the yogurt and chilies and bring to a boil, then cover and simmer for 10 minutes.

Add the pieces of fish and continue to simmer for 10–12 minutes or until the fish flakes easily and is cooked through. Do not overcook or the fish will give off liquid and the sauce will separate.

Garnish with cilantro leaves and serve immediately. If you let the dish sit, the fish may give off liquid and make the sauce more runny.

Knobbly ginger "hands" are familiar to most cooks today, but it can still be surprising to discover that the plant has been cultivated for millennia in China. Thought to be indigenous to northern India, ginger is used extensively in Chinese, Indian, and Asian cooking for its sweet aroma and peppery, tangy flavor. It is featured in soups, curries, salads, and in relishes for its clean, digestive qualities. When buying, look for plump examples with pink-beige skin. The flesh inside should be moist and creamy-lemon. Ginger is also available dried, ground, and pickled.

burmese chicken curry

serves 6

NOT SURPRISINGLY FOR A COUNTRY BORDERED BY FIVE OTHER COUNTRIES, THE CUISINE OF BURMA (MYANMAR) SHOWS VARIOUS OUTSIDE INFLUENCES—IN PARTICULAR THAI, INDIAN, AND CHINESE. BURMESE CURRIES ARE GENERALLY NOT AS SPICY AS INDIAN ONES, THOUGH THEY SHARE A LOVE OF AROMATIC FLAVORS.

Indian curry powder, medium-spiced	1 tablespoon
garam masala	1 teaspoon
cayenne pepper	1/2 teaspoon
sweet paprika	2 teaspoons
chicken	3 pounds 8 ounces, cut into eight pieces or mixed chicken pieces
onions	2, chopped
garlic	3 cloves, crushed
ginger	2 teaspoons grated
tomatoes	2, chopped
tomato paste	2 teaspoons
lemongrass	1 stem, white part only, thinly sliced
oil	3 tablespoons
chicken stock	2 cups
sugar	1/2 teaspoon
fish sauce	1 tablespoon

Mix the curry powder, garam masala, cayenne pepper, and paprika in a bowl. Rub this spice mix all over the chicken pieces and set aside.

Combine the onions, garlic, ginger, tomatoes, tomato paste, and lemongrass in a food processor or in a mortar with a pestle. Process or pound to a smooth paste.

In a large, heavy-based frying pan (that will fit the chicken pieces in a single layer), heat the oil over medium heat. Add the chicken and brown all over, then remove from the pan. In the same frying pan, add the onion paste and cook over low heat for 5–8 minutes, stirring constantly. Put the chicken back into the pan and coat in the paste.

Add the stock and sugar and bring to a simmer. Reduce the heat to low, cover, and cook for 1 1/4 hours or until the chicken is very tender. While cooking, skim and discard any oil that surfaces. Stir in the fish sauce and serve.

Rub the spice mixture well into the chicken pieces.

Process or pound the paste ingredients until smooth.

beef rendang .... serves 6

IN THIS FESTIVE DISH OF INDONESIA AND MALAYSIA, BEEF IS COOKED UNTIL TENDER AND COATED IN A RICH, THICK SAUCE, PERMEATED WITH THE WARM, COMPLEX AROMA AND FLAVOR OF SPICES AND SEASONINGS. JUSTIFIABLY POPULAR, IT IS ALSO EASY TO MAKE, WITH EVERYTHING GOING INTO THE ONE POT.

beef chuck	3 pounds 5 ounces
onions	2, roughly chopped
garlic	2 cloves, crushed
unsweetened coconut milk	14 fluid-ounce can, or 1²/₃ cups
ground coriander	2 teaspoons
ground fennel	½ teaspoon
ground cumin	2 teaspoons
ground cloves	¼ teaspoon
red chilies	4–6, chopped
lemon juice	1 tablespoon
lemongrass	1 stem, white part only, cut lengthwise
jaggery	2 teaspoons shaved (or 2 teaspoons brown sugar)

Trim the meat of any excess fat or sinew and cut into 1¼-inch cubes. Put the onion and garlic in a food processor or in a mortar with a pestle, and process or pound to a smooth paste.

Put the coconut milk in a large saucepan and bring to a boil, then reduce the heat to medium and cook, stirring occasionally, for 15 minutes or until the milk reduces by half and the oil separates. Do not allow the milk to brown.

Add the coriander, fennel, cumin, and cloves to the pan, and stir for 1 minute. Add the meat and cook for 2 minutes or until it changes color. Add the onion mixture, chilies, lemon juice, lemongrass, and jaggery. Cook covered over medium heat for 2 hours or until the liquid reduces and the mixture thickens. Stir frequently to prevent it sticking to the bottom of the pan.

Uncover and continue cooking until the oil from the coconut milk begins to emerge again, letting the curry develop color and flavor. Be careful that it does not burn. The curry is cooked when it is brown and dry.

Simmer the coconut milk until the oil "splits"—it separates.

Add the spices to the coconut milk and cook until fragrant.

lamb dhansak . . . . serves 6

THIS SUMPTUOUS CURRY COMES FROM THE PARSIS OF WEST INDIA, WHO EMIGRATED THERE FROM IRAN IN THE SEVENTH CENTURY. IT IS STRIKING FOR THE NUMBER OF DIFFERENT LENTILS USED, AS WELL AS VARIOUS SPICES, TENDER LAMB, AND VEGETABLES SUCH AS SPINACH, WINTER SQUASH, AND EGGPLANT.

yellow lentils	3/4 cup
dried yellow mung beans	2 teaspoons
dried chickpeas	2 tablespoons
red lentils	3 tablespoons
eggplant	1, unpeeled
winter squash	1 small wedge (about 5 1/2 ounces), unpeeled
ghee or oil	2 tablespoons
onion	1, finely chopped
garlic	3 cloves, crushed
ginger	1 tablespoon grated
boneless leg or shoulder of lamb	2 pounds 4 ounces, cut into 1 1/4-inch cubes
cinnamon stick	1
cardamom pods	5, bruised
cloves	3
ground coriander	1 tablespoon
ground turmeric	1 teaspoon
chili powder	1 teaspoon or to taste
spinach or amaranth	1 3/4 cups, cut into 2-inch lengths
tomatoes	2, halved
long green chilies	2, split lengthwise, seeded
lime juice	3 tablespoons

Soak the yellow lentils, yellow mung beans, and chickpeas in water for about 2 hours, then drain well.

Combine all four types of legumes in a saucepan, add 4 cups water, cover, and bring to a boil. Uncover and simmer for 15 minutes, skimming any film that forms on the surface. Stir occasionally to make sure all the legumes cook at the same rate and are soft. Drain and lightly mash to a similar texture.

Cook the eggplant and squash in boiling water for 10–15 minutes or until soft. Scoop out the flesh from the squash and cut it into pieces. Peel the eggplant carefully (it may be very pulpy) and cut the flesh into small pieces.

Heat the ghee or oil in a flameproof casserole dish or karahi (see note below). Fry the onion, garlic, and ginger for 5 minutes or until lightly browned and softened. Add the lamb and brown for 10 minutes or until aromatic. Add the cinnamon, cardamom pods, cloves, coriander, turmeric, and chili powder, and fry for 5 minutes to allow the flavors to develop. Add 2/3 cup water, cover, and simmer for 40 minutes or until the lamb is tender.

Add the mashed legumes, eggplant, squash, spinach or amaranth, tomatoes, and chilies to the pan. Add the lime juice and simmer for 15 minutes (if the sauce is too thick, add a little water). Stir well, then check the seasoning. The dhansak should be flavorsome, aromatic, tart, and spicy.

Note: A karahi is a deep, wok-shaped cooking dish used in Indian and Balti cooking. It lends itself perfectly to one-pot meals and can be taken straight from the stove to the table for serving.

spicy shrimp . . . . serves 4–6

TURMERIC IS AT THE HEART OF SO MANY CURRIES. IT IMPARTS NOT JUST COLOR, BUT ALSO A SUBTLE AROMA AND EARTHY, SLIGHTLY BITTER FLAVOR. USING GROUND TURMERIC IS EASY AND CONVENIENT BUT BUY FRESH TURMERIC ROOT IF YOU SEE IT. IT LOOKS SIMILAR TO OLD GINGER, BUT IS WONDERFULLY GOLDEN INSIDE.

raw shrimp	2 pounds 4 ounces, peeled, deveined, tails intact (reserve shells and heads)
ground turmeric	1 teaspoon
oil	3 tablespoons
onions	2, finely chopped
garlic	4–6 cloves, crushed
green chilies	1–2, seeded, chopped
ground cumin	2 teaspoons
ground coriander	2 teaspoons
paprika	1 teaspoon
plain yogurt	1/3 cup
thickened whipping cream	1/3 cup
cilantro	1 large handful leaves, chopped

Bring 4 cups water to a boil in a saucepan. Add the reserved shrimp shells and heads, then reduce the heat and simmer for 2 minutes. Skim any film that forms on the surface during cooking. Strain, discard the shells and heads, and return the liquid to the pan. You will need about 3 cups liquid (add water if necessary). Add the turmeric and peeled shrimp. Cook for 1 minute or until the shrimp just turn pink, then remove the shrimp. Reserve the stock.

Heat the oil in a large saucepan. Add the onion and cook over medium heat, stirring, for 8 minutes or until lightly golden brown. Add the garlic and chilies and cook for 1–2 minutes. Then add the cumin, coriander, and paprika. Stirring, cook for 1–2 minutes or until fragrant.

Gradually add the reserved stock, bring to a boil and cook, stirring occasionally, for 30–35 minutes or until the mixture reduces by half and thickens. Remove from the heat and stir in the yogurt. Add the shrimp and stir over low heat for 2–3 minutes or until the shrimp are warmed through. Do not boil. Stir in the cream and cilantro leaves. Cover and leave for 15 minutes to allow the flavors to infuse. Reheat gently and serve.

Simmer the shrimp shells and heads, skimming the surface.

Poach the shrimp in the stock until just pink and curled.

Gradually add the reserved shrimp stock to the saucepan.

beef and mustard seed curry . . . . serves 6

AFTER YOU FRY THE SPICES, THIS COMFORTING CURRY COOKS ITSELF. STAY CLOSE WHILE COOKING THE SPICES TO ENSURE THAT THEY DO NOT BURN. THE MUSTARD SEEDS IN PARTICULAR GIVE THIS DISH A DISTINCTIVE FLAVOR—HEATING THEM UNTIL THEY POP BRINGS OUT THEIR PLEASANT NUTTY TASTE.

oil	3 tablespoons
brown mustard seeds	2 tablespoons
dried red chilies	4
yellow split peas	1 tablespoon
French shallots	2 cups thinly sliced
garlic	8 cloves, crushed
ginger	1 tablespoon finely grated
curry leaves	15
ground turmeric	1/2 teaspoon
tomatoes	2 cups, canned, chopped
beef chuck	2 pounds 4 ounces, diced
beef stock	1 3/4 cups

In a heavy-based saucepan over medium heat, add the oil, mustard seeds, chilies, and split peas. As soon as the mustard seeds start to pop, add the shallots, garlic, ginger, curry leaves, and turmeric. Cook for 5 minutes, then add the tomato, beef, and stock.

Bring to a boil, then reduce to a simmer, cover, and cook for 2 hours or until the beef is very tender and the sauce reduces. While cooking, skim and discard any oil that surfaces.

Shiny, dark-green curry leaves are from a tropical evergreen tree native to Sri Lanka and India. The tree is a relative of the lemon tree, and shares its lingering citrusy, slightly spicy aroma. Fresh curry leaves are used widely in southern Indian, Sri Lankan, and Malay cooking. When added whole to dishes, the leaves are first cooked in oil to extract their aroma and distinct flavor, then discarded at the end and not eaten. They are also used as a garnish. Keep fresh leaves in the refrigerator. If buying dried leaves, choose ones that have retained their green color.

three ways with coconut

THE COCONUT PALM GROWS ALL OVER ASIA AND SUCH IS THE IMPORTANCE OF THE FRUIT THAT IT IS KNOWN AS *SHRIFAL* OR "FRUIT OF LUSTER" IN PARTS OF INDIA. COUNTLESS CURRIES ARE BASED AROUND COCONUT MILK OR CREAM, WHICH ARE ALSO USED IN SOUPS, SALADS, AND PASTRIES. THE DRIED FLESH IS USED IN GARNISHES, CHUTNEYS, RAITAS, AND DESSERTS. WHEN SERVED ALONGSIDE OR AFTER A SPICY CURRY, COCONUT SIDES AND DRINKS CAN EITHER SOOTHE AND REFRESH PALATES OR ADD A LITTLE EXTRA SPICINESS TO THE MAIN EVENT.

coconut and cilantro chutney

Combine 1³/₄ cups roughly chopped cilantro (including the roots), ¼ cup dried coconut, 1 tablespoon soft brown sugar, 1 tablespoon grated ginger, 1 chopped small onion, 2 tablespoons lemon juice, 1–2 seeded green chilies, and 1 teaspoon salt in a food processor. Process for 1 minute, or until finely chopped. Refrigerate until ready to serve. Numerous variations of this chutney are served, depending on the region and tastes. Try substituting 1 handful roughly chopped mint leaves for the cilantro in this recipe, or add 5 chopped scallions, including the green part, instead of the onion. If you prefer more fire in your chutney, do not remove the seeds from the chilies. Serves 4.

coconut and pineapple cooler

Peel and chop 2 pineapples and extract the juice using a juicer. Transfer the pineapple juice to a large pitcher and stir in 2 cups coconut milk. Pour 1 cup of the mixture into sixteen holes of an ice-cube tray and freeze. Chill the remaining mixture. When the ice cubes have frozen, pour the juice mixture into four glasses, add the ice cubes, and garnish with mint and pineapple leaves. Serves 4.

fresh coconut chutney

Soak 1 teaspoon chana dal (gram lentils) and 1 teaspoon urad dal (black lentils) in cold water for 2 hours, then drain well. Combine the grated flesh from ½ fresh coconut, 2 seeded and chopped green chilies, and ½ teaspoon salt in a food processor or in a mortar with a pestle. Process or pound to a smooth paste. Heat 1 tablespoon oil in a small saucepan and add 1 teaspoon black mustard seeds and the dals, then cover and shake the pan until they pop. Add 5 curry leaves and fry for 1 minute or until the dal browns. Add these ingredients to the coconut with 1 teaspoon tamarind puree and mix well. Serves 4.

coconut and cilantro chutney

onion bhaji curry

THESE BHAJIS GET THEIR DISTINCTIVE TASTE AND COLOR FROM NUTTY-TASTING, YELLOW CHICKPEA FLOUR AND TURMERIC. THEY ALSO CONTAIN ASAFETIDA, A DRIED RESIN WITH A PUNGENT AROMA THAT HAS EARNED IT THE NAME DEVIL'S DUNG. IT IS WIDELY USED IN INDIA TO FLAVOR DISHES AND FOR ITS MEDICINAL PROPERTIES.

oil	2 tablespoons
ginger	1 teaspoon grated
garlic	2 cloves, crushed
crushed tomatoes	15-ounces can
ground turmeric	1/4 teaspoon
chili powder	1/2 teaspoon
ground cumin	1 1/2 teaspoons
ground coriander	1 teaspoon
garam masala	1 1/2 tablespoons
whipping cream	1 cup
cilantro	chopped leaves, to serve

bhajis

chickpea flour	1 1/4 cups
ground turmeric	1/4 teaspoon
chili powder	1/2 teaspoon
asafetida	1/4 teaspoon
onion	1, thinly sliced
oil	for deep-frying

Heat the oil in a frying pan, add the ginger and garlic, and cook for 2 minutes or until fragrant. Add the tomatoes, turmeric, chili powder, cumin, coriander, and 1 cup water. Bring to a boil, then reduce the heat and simmer for 5 minutes or until thickened slightly. Add the garam masala, then stir in the cream and simmer for 1–2 minutes. Remove from the heat.

To make the bhajis, combine the chickpea flour, turmeric, chili powder, and asafetida with 1/2 cup water, and season with salt. Whisk to make a smooth batter. Stir in the onion and coat with the batter.

Fill a deep, heavy-based saucepan one-third full of oil and heat to 315°F or until a cube of bread dropped into the oil browns in 30 seconds. Add spoonfuls of the onion mixture in batches and cook for 1–2 minutes or until golden brown, then drain on paper towels. Pour the sauce over the bhajis and garnish with the cilantro leaves.

Coat the sliced onion well in the smooth batter.

Deep-fry spoonfuls of the bhaji mixture until crisp and golden.

malaysian chicken curry .... serves 4–6

MALAYSIAN CUISINE IS AN EXCITING MIX OF OUTSIDE INFLUENCES—FROM THAI TO EUROPEAN—WITH ITS OWN, OFTEN HIGHLY REGIONAL, DISTINCTIVE CHARACTERISTICS. MALAYSIAN CURRIES OFTEN DRAW ON THE SPICES OF INDIA AND THE SEASONINGS OF THAI CURRIES, BLENDING THEM WITH SHRIMP PASTE, COCONUT MILK, CHILIES, AND CANDLENUTS.

dried shrimp	3 teaspoons
oil	1/3 cup
red chilies	6–8, seeded, finely chopped
garlic	4 cloves, crushed
lemongrass	3 stems, white part only, finely chopped
ground turmeric	2 teaspoons
candlenuts	10
onions	2 large, chopped
unsweetened coconut milk	1 cup
whole chicken	3 pounds 5 ounces, cut into eight pieces
unsweetened coconut cream	1/2 cup
lime juice	2 tablespoons

Put the dried shrimp in a frying pan and dry-fry over low heat, shaking the pan regularly for 3 minutes or until the shrimp are dark orange and are giving off a strong aroma. Allow to cool.

Combine the shrimp, half the oil, chilies, garlic, lemongrass, turmeric, and candlenuts in a food processor or in a mortar with a pestle. Process or pound to a smooth paste.

Heat the remaining oil in a wok or frying pan, and add the onion and 1/4 teaspoon salt. Stirring regularly, cook over low-medium heat for 8 minutes or until golden. Add the spice paste and stir for 5 minutes. If the mixture begins to stick to the bottom of the pan, add 2 tablespoons coconut milk. It is important to cook the mixture thoroughly, as this develops the flavors.

Add the chicken to the wok or pan. Stirring, cook for 5 minutes or until it begins to brown. Stir in the coconut milk and 1 cup water, and bring to a boil. Reduce the heat and simmer for 50 minutes or until the chicken is cooked and the sauce thickens slightly. Pour in the coconut cream and bring the mixture back to a boil, stirring constantly. Add the lime juice and serve immediately.

Dry-fry the shrimp until dark orange and aromatic.

If using a food processor, scrape down the sides of the bowl.

spinach koftas
in yogurt sauce . . . . serves 4

GUJARATI DISHES SUCH AS THIS ARE UNIQUE IN INDIA IN THAT THEY ARE NEARLY ALWAYS VEGETARIAN. THOUGH SOUTHERN GUJARATI CUISINE HAS A PENCHANT FOR GREEN CHILIES, THESE CURRIES ARE TYPICALLY MILD, RELYING ON FRESH VEGETABLES, YOGURT, AND ACCOMPANYING PICKLES AND CHUTNEYS FOR EXTRA SPICE.

yogurt sauce

plain yogurt	1 1/2 cups
chickpea flour	1/3 cup
oil	1 tablespoon
black mustard seeds	2 teaspoons
fenugreek seeds	1 teaspoon
curry leaves	6
onion	1 large, finely chopped
garlic	3 cloves, crushed
ground turmeric	1 teaspoon
chili powder	1/2 teaspoon

koftas

spinach	1 bunch (about 1 pound), leaves picked off the stems
chickpea flour	1 1/2 cups
red onion	1, finely chopped
tomato	1 ripe, finely diced
garlic	2 cloves, crushed
ground cumin	1 teaspoon
cilantro	2 tablespoons chopped leaves
oil	for deep-frying
cilantro	leaves, to serve

To make the yogurt sauce, whisk the yogurt, chickpea flour, and 3 cups water until a smooth paste.

Heat the oil in a heavy-based saucepan or deep-frying pan over low heat. Add the mustard and fenugreek seeds, and the curry leaves. Cover and allow the seeds to pop for 1 minute. Add the onion and cook for 5 minutes or until soft and starting to brown.

Add the garlic and stir for 1 minute or until soft. Add the turmeric and chili powder and stir for 30 seconds. Add the yogurt mixture, bring to a boil, then reduce the heat and simmer over low heat for 10 minutes.

To make the spinach koftas, blanch the spinach in boiling water for 1 minute. Refresh in cold water and drain. Squeeze out any extra water by putting the spinach in a colander and pressing it against the side with a spoon. Finely chop the spinach. Combine with the remaining kofta ingredients and up to 3 tablespoons water, a little at a time, adding enough water to make the mixture soft but not sloppy. If it becomes too sloppy, add more chickpea flour. Shape the mixture into balls by rolling it in dampened hands, using about 1 tablespoon of mixture for each. This should make 12 koftas.

Fill a heavy-based saucepan one-third full with oil and heat to 350°F or until a cube of bread browns in 15 seconds. Lower the koftas into the oil in batches and fry until golden and crisp. Don't crowd the pan. Remove the koftas as they cook, shake off any excess oil, and add them to the yogurt sauce. Gently reheat the yogurt sauce, garnish with the cilantro leaves, and serve.

dal... serves 4–6

IN INDIA, DAL REFERS TO BOTH THE DRIED LEGUMES AND THE FINISHED DISH. IN THIS RECIPE, LENTILS ARE USED, BUT CHICKPEAS AND OTHER BEANS AND PEAS ARE ALSO POPULAR. TO BOLSTER THE SIMPLE FLAVOR OF THE LENTILS, SPICES SUCH AS CUMIN AND ASAFETIDA ARE FRIED IN GHEE, RELEASING THEIR EARTHY AROMAS.

red lentils	3/4 cup
ginger	3 thick slices
ground turmeric	1/2 teaspoon
ghee or oil	1 tablespoon
garlic	2 cloves, crushed
onion	1, finely chopped
yellow mustard seeds	1/2 teaspoon
asafetida	pinch, optional
cumin seeds	1 teaspoon
ground coriander	1 teaspoon
green chilies	2, halved lengthwise
lemon juice	2 tablespoons

Put the lentils and 3 cups water in a saucepan, and bring to a boil. Reduce the heat, and add the ginger and turmeric. Simmer covered for 20 minutes or until the lentils are tender. Stir occasionally to prevent the lentils from sticking to the pan. Remove the ginger and season the lentil mixture with salt.

Heat the ghee or oil in a frying pan, add the garlic, onion, and mustard seeds. Cook over medium heat for 5 minutes or until the onion is golden. Add the asafetida, cumin seeds, ground coriander, and chilies, and cook for 2 minutes.

Add the onion mixture to the lentils and stir gently to combine. Add 1/2 cup water, reduce the heat to low, and cook for 5 minutes. Stir in the lemon juice and serve.

Add the ginger slices and turmeric to the lentils and simmer.

Cook the onion, mustard seeds, and garlic until the onion is golden.

Stir the onion mixture gently through the lentil mixture.

jungle curry shrimp .... serves 6

BE WARNED: JUNGLE CURRIES ARE GENERALLY HOT CURRIES! TRADITIONALLY, NO COCONUT IS USED TO ABSORB THE HEAT OF THE CHILIES. HOWEVER, THESE CURRIES USUALLY ALSO FEATURE PLENTY OF FRESH SPICES AND VEGETABLES, AS IS THE CASE HERE. THE FINAL FLAVOR IS AROMATIC, HOT, AND SALTY, BUT NOT SCORCHING.

jungle curry paste

dried red chilies	10–12
white pepper	1 teaspoon
red Asian shallots	4
garlic	4 cloves
lemongrass	1 stem, white part only, chopped
galangal	1 tablespoon finely chopped
cilantro	2 roots
ginger	1 tablespoon finely chopped
shrimp paste	1 tablespoon dry-roasted
peanut oil	1 tablespoon
garlic	1 clove, crushed
fish sauce	1 tablespoon
candlenuts	8, ground
fish stock	1¼ cups
whiskey	1 tablespoon
Kaffir lime leaves	3, torn
raw shrimp	1 pound 5 ounces peeled, deveined, tails intact
carrot	1 small, quartered lengthwise, sliced thinly diagonally
yard-long beans	2 cups cut into ¾-inch lengths
bamboo shoots	¼ cup canned, sliced, drained
Thai basil leaves	to serve

Soak the chilies in boiling water for 5 minutes or until soft. Remove the stem and seeds, then chop. Put the chilies and the remaining curry paste ingredients in a food processor or in a mortar with a pestle. Process or pound to a smooth paste. Add a little water if it is too thick.

Heat a wok over medium heat, add the oil, and swirl to coat. Add the garlic and 3 tablespoons of the curry paste. Stirring, cook for 5 minutes. Add the fish sauce, ground candlenuts, stock, whiskey, lime leaves, shrimp, carrot, beans, and bamboo shoots. Bring to a boil, then reduce the heat and simmer for 5 minutes or until the shrimp and vegetables are cooked. Top with the basil leaves and serve.

sri lankan fried pork curry . . . . serves 6

THIS CURRY IS INTERESTING FOR THE NUMBER OF FLAVORINGS NOT OFTEN SEEN IN WESTERN DISHES. FENUGREEK SEEDS ARE SMALL, HARD, AND OCHER-COLORED. THEY ARE POWERFULLY SCENTED AND HAVE A BITTER TASTE, THOUGH THIS SOFTENS ON COOKING.

oil	1/3 cup
boned pork shoulder	2 pounds 12 ounces, cut into 1 1/4-inch cubes
red onion	1 large, finely chopped
garlic	3–4 cloves, crushed
ginger	1 tablespoon grated
curry leaves	10
fenugreek seeds	1/2 teaspoon
chili powder	1/2 teaspoon
cardamom pods	6, bruised
Sri Lankan curry powder	2 1/2 tablespoons
white vinegar	1 tablespoon
tamarind concentrate	3 tablespoons
unsweetened coconut cream	1 cup

Heat half the oil in a large saucepan over high heat. Add the meat and cook in batches for 6 minutes or until well browned. Remove from the pan. Heat the remaining oil, add the onion, and cook over medium heat for 5 minutes or until lightly browned. Add the garlic and ginger, and cook for 2 minutes. Stir in the curry leaves, spices, and curry powder, and cook for 2 minutes or until fragrant. Stir in the vinegar and 1 teaspoon salt.

Return the browned meat to the pan, and add the tamarind concentrate and 1 1/4 cups water. Stirring occasionally, simmer covered for 40–50 minutes or until the meat is tender. Stir in the coconut cream and simmer uncovered for 15 minutes or until the sauce reduces and thickens a little. Serve immediately.

The tropical tamarind tree is prized for its fruit pods, each containing a sticky, fleshy acidic pulp wrapped around small, shiny, dark brown seeds. The tree is indigenous to east Africa but it flourishes wild in India, where the pulp is greatly appreciated for its refreshing sweet–sour taste and fruity aroma. Across tropical Asia it serves as an excellent souring agent, and is used in soups, curries, chutneys, drinks, and sweetmeats. In the West, its main use is in Worcestershire sauce. Tamarind is sold as a concentrated paste in jars, or in blocks or cakes that still contain the seeds. Store both in the refrigerator for up to one year.

rogan josh

THIS CLASSIC, SUPERBLY AROMATIC, SLOW-COOKING CURRY ORIGINATED IN PERSIA, AND TRAVELED TO KASHMIR IN INDIA'S FAR NORTH, UNDER THE MOGUL EMPIRE. IN KASHMIR IT WAS ADAPTED AND PERFECTED, INCORPORATING THE LOCAL CHILIES, SAFFRON, AND CARDAMOM.

garlic	8 cloves, crushed
ginger	3 teaspoons grated
ground cumin	2 teaspoons
chili powder	1 teaspoon
paprika	2 teaspoons
ground coriander	2 teaspoons
boneless leg or shoulder of lamb	2 pounds 4 ounces, cut into 1¼-inch cubes
ghee or oil	3 tablespoons
onion	1, finely chopped
cardamom pods	6, bruised
cloves	4
Indian bay (cassia) leaves	2
cinnamon stick	1
Greek-style yogurt	¾ cup (or plain yogurt drained in cheesecloth)
saffron	4 threads, mixed with 2 tablespoons milk
garam masala	¼ teaspoon

Combine the garlic, ginger, cumin, chili powder, paprika, and coriander in a large bowl. Add the meat and stir thoroughly to coat the meat cubes well. Cover and marinate for at least 2 hours, or overnight, in the refrigerator.

Heat the ghee or oil in a flameproof casserole dish or karahi over low heat. Add the onion and cook for about 10 minutes or until the onion is lightly browned. Remove from the dish.

Add the cardamom pods, cloves, bay leaves, and cinnamon stick to the dish and fry for 1 minute. Increase the heat to high, add the meat and onion, then mix well and fry for 2 minutes. Stir well, then reduce the heat to low, cover, and cook for 15 minutes. Uncover and fry for another 3–5 minutes or until the meat is quite dry. Add ½ cup water, cover, and cook for 5–7 minutes or until the water evaporates and the oil separates out and floats on the surface. Fry the meat for another 1–2 minutes, then add 1 cup water. Cover and cook for 40–50 minutes, gently simmering until the meat is tender. The liquid will reduce quite a bit.

Stir in the yogurt when the meat is tender, taking care not to allow the meat to catch on the base of the dish. Add the saffron and milk. Stir the mixture a few times to mix in the saffron. Season with salt. Remove from the heat and sprinkle with the garam masala.

Coat the meat well in the mixed spices and leave to marinate.

Cook the onion until lightly browned and remove from pan.

Dry-fry the spices for 1 minute or until they become aromatic.

sri lankan eggplant curry .... serves 6

INDIAN AND SRI LANKAN COOKING HAVE MANY SIMILARITIES, BUT IT WOULD BE WRONG TO THINK THEY ARE INTERCHANGEABLE. CRUCIALLY, THEIR CURRY POWDERS DIFFER. SRI LANKAN CURRY POWDER IS MADE BY ROASTING SPICES SUCH AS CUMIN, FENNEL, AND CORIANDER, AND HAS A DARK, INTENSE FLAVOR.

ground turmeric	1 teaspoon
slender eggplants	12, cut into 1½-inch rounds
oil	for deep-frying, plus 2 tablespoons extra
onions	2, finely chopped
Sri Lankan curry powder	2 tablespoons
garlic	2 cloves, crushed
curry leaves	8, roughly chopped, plus extra whole leaves for garnish
chili powder	½ teaspoon
unsweetened coconut cream	1 cup

Mix half the ground turmeric with 1 teaspoon salt and rub into the eggplant, ensuring the cut surfaces are well coated. Put in a colander and leave for 1 hour. Rinse well and put on crumpled paper towels to remove any excess moisture.

Fill a deep, heavy-based saucepan one-third full of oil and heat to 350°F or until a cube of bread browns in the oil in 15 seconds. Cook the eggplant in batches for 1 minute or until golden brown. Drain on crumpled paper towels.

Heat the extra oil in a large saucepan, add the onion, and cook over medium heat for 5 minutes or until browned. Add the curry powder, garlic, curry leaves, chili powder, eggplants, and remaining turmeric to the pan. Cook for 2 minutes. Stir in the coconut cream and 1 cup water, and season with salt to taste. Reduce the heat and simmer over low heat for 3 minutes or until the eggplant is fully cooked and the sauce thickens slightly. Garnish with extra curry leaves.

Rub the ground turmeric and salt into the eggplants' cut surfaces.

Cook the eggplants in a deep saucepan until golden and tender.

curried squid

THIS QUICK AND SIMPLE CURRY PACKS QUITE A FLAVOR PUNCH. IT FEATURES THE ROUND, EARTHY FLAVORS OF CUMIN AND TURMERIC, ALONGSIDE THE FRESH, SHARPER FLAVORS OF CHILI, GINGER, AND LIME JUICE. VERSIONS OF THIS DISH ARE EATEN THROUGHOUT TROPICAL THAILAND, SINGAPORE, AND MALAYSIA.

squid	2 pounds 4 ounces
cumin seeds	1 teaspoon
coriander seeds	1 teaspoon
chili powder	1 teaspoon
ground turmeric	1/2 teaspoon
oil	2 tablespoons
onion	1, finely chopped
curry leaves	10, plus extra for garnish
fenugreek seeds	1/2 teaspoon
garlic	4 cloves, crushed
ginger	2 3/4-inch piece, grated
unsweetened coconut cream	1/2 cup
lime juice	3 tablespoons

Pull the squid heads and tentacles out of their bodies, along with any innards, and discard them. Peel off the skins. Rinse the bodies well, pulling out the clear quills, then cut the bodies into 1-inch rings.

Dry-fry the cumin and coriander seeds in a frying pan over medium–high heat for 2–3 minutes or until fragrant. Allow to cool. Using a mortar with a pestle or a spice grinder, crush or grind to a powder. Mix the ground cumin and coriander with the chili powder and turmeric. Add the squid and mix well.

In a heavy-based frying pan, heat the oil and fry the onion until lightly browned. Add the curry leaves, fenugreek, garlic, ginger, and coconut cream. Bring slowly to a boil. Add the squid, then stir well. Simmer for 2–3 minutes or until cooked and tender. Stir in the lime juice, season, and serve garnished with curry leaves.

Wonderfully tangy and aromatic, limes are native to the tropics (possibly originating in Malaysia), where they are used widely in cooking. They are valued as a souring agent and are added to innumerable curries and stews, and are particularly good in dipping sauces, chutneys, and pickles, some of which can be quite sharp. It is not difficult to make your own lime pickles, but ready-made pickled limes are easily bought from Asian food stores. To get the maximum flavor impact from fresh limes, squeeze them only as needed—for this reason, too, the juice is generally added to a dish only at the end of cooking.

hot and sour

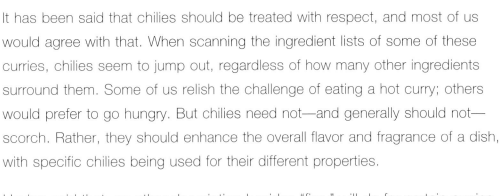

It has been said that chilies should be treated with respect, and most of us would agree with that. When scanning the ingredient lists of some of these curries, chilies seem to jump out, regardless of how many other ingredients surround them. Some of us relish the challenge of eating a hot curry; others would prefer to go hungry. But chilies need not—and generally should not—scorch. Rather, they should enhance the overall flavor and fragrance of a dish, with specific chilies being used for their different properties.

Having said that, no other description besides "fiery" will do for certain curries. The jungle curries of Thailand, for example, some of Goa's seafood curries, and many Malaysian and Balinese curries fall into this category. Traders introduced chilies to Southeast Asia and India in the sixteenth century. These spicy dishes can reflect an area's mixed heritage. Goa's notoriously hot vindaloo curry began life as a vinegar and pork dish of the Portuguese, and the Nonya cooking of Malaysia, a mix of indigenous and Chinese cooking, is famous for its hot, tangy, and aromatic curries.

If venturing into this taste arena for the first time, just remember that the active agent in chilies, capsaicin, is found mostly in the ribs and seeds of chilies. So, seeding a chili is a fail-safe way of reducing heat levels. Otherwise, use less than the recipe specifies—you can always add more. As a general guide, the smaller the chili, the hotter it will be. As well, have plain rice, yogurt, and chilled beer on standby when eating chili-based dishes.

Chilies are not the only ingredient adding heat to a curry. Mustard seeds and peppercorns can also be extremely potent. But, as with chilies, searing heat is generally not the aim—both of these spices offer a warm, biting flavor and aroma that blend well with other fresh and dried spices and herbs. In particular, hot curries invite the use of sour flavors such as tamarind, tart vinegar, yogurt, and crisp, clean lime juice and lemongrass. The combination of hot and sour is a particularly happy one, with the sour elements adding an extra layer of flavor and fragrance to a hot dish. Sour ingredients also include a number of vegetables—such as bitter melon and Thai apple eggplants—that add textural interest. Even further complexity is added with the use of rich, creamy coconut milk. As with all curries, balance is the key.

pork vindaloo .... serves 4

THE PORTUGUESE FIRST INTRODUCED THIS PORK, GARLIC, AND VINEGAR STEW TO GOA. THE LOCALS ADOPTED IT BUT, FINDING IT LACKING SLIGHTLY IN FLAVOR, ADAPTED IT BY ADDING SPICES, EXTRA GARLIC, AND A HEFTY QUANTITY OF CHILIES. THE RESULT IS VINDALOO, FAMED——OR FEARED——FOR ITS HEAT AND SPICINESS.

pork fillet	2 pounds 4 ounces
oil	3 tablespoons
onions	2, finely chopped
garlic	4 cloves, crushed
ginger	1 tablespoon finely chopped
garam masala	1 tablespoon
brown mustard seeds	2 teaspoons
ready-made vindaloo paste	4 tablespoons

Trim the pork of any excess fat and sinew and cut it into bite-sized pieces.

Heat the oil in a saucepan, add the meat in small batches, and cook over medium heat for 5–7 minutes, or until browned. Remove from the pan.

Add the onion, garlic, ginger, garam masala, and mustard seeds to the pan. Stirring, cook for 5 minutes or until the onion is soft.

Return all the meat to the pan, add the vindaloo paste, and cook, stirring, for 2 minutes. Add 2½ cups water and bring to a boil. Reduce the heat and simmer covered for 1½ hours or until the meat is tender.

Mustard seeds are available in three main varieties: black, the hottest and most pungent; brown; and white (sometimes called yellow). Mustard has been cultivated for thousands of years and is eaten today in various forms all over the world. In India, in particular, mustard is considered an auspicious ingredient. Whole mustard seeds have little scent—it is only when mixed with a liquid such as water that the seeds release their distinctive aroma and sharp, biting flavor. When fried in oil until they pop, as is common in Indian curry preparations, the seeds take on a nutty taste without the searing heat. Mustard seeds are also available as a paste, powder, and oil.

balinese seafood curry

THE CHILI ARRIVED IN BALI RELATIVELY RECENTLY—WITH THE PORTUGUESE IN THE SIXTEENTH CENTURY—BUT IT HAS FOUND ITS WAY INTO MOST DISHES. BALINESE CUISINE IS RENOWNED FOR ITS SPICY AND COMPLEX FLAVORS, ITS USE OF FISH, AND ITS CAREFUL PREPARATION OF THE SPICE BLEND.

curry paste

shrimp paste	1 teaspoon
coriander seeds	1 tablespoon
tomatoes	2
red chilies	5
garlic	5 cloves, crushed
lemongrass	2 stems, white part only, chopped
ground almonds	1 tablespoon
ground nutmeg	1/4 teaspoon
ground turmeric	1 teaspoon
tamarind puree	1/4 cup

lime juice	3 tablespoons
skinless, firm white fish fillets	9 ounces, cut into 1 1/4-inch cubes
oil	3 tablespoons
red onions	2, chopped
red chilies	2, seeded, sliced
raw shrimp	14 ounces, peeled, deveined, tails intact
squid tubes	9 ounces, cut into 1/2-inch rings
fish stock	1/2 cup
Thai basil leaves	shredded, to serve

Wrap the shrimp paste in foil and dry-fry it with the coriander seeds in a frying pan over medium-high heat for 2–3 minutes or until fragrant. Allow to cool. Using a mortar with a pestle or a spice grinder, crush or grind the coriander seeds to a powder. Process the shrimp in a small food processor until it becomes very finely shredded—forming a "floss."

Score a cross in the base of the tomatoes, place in a heatproof bowl, and cover with boiling water. Leave to sit for 30 seconds, then transfer to cold water and peel the skin away from the cross. Cut the tomatoes in half and scoop out the seeds. Discard the seeds and roughly chop the tomato flesh.

Combine the crushed coriander seeds, the shredded shrimp, and the tomatoes with the remaining curry paste ingredients in a food processor or in a mortar with a pestle. Process or pound to a smooth paste.

Put the lime juice in a bowl and season with salt and freshly ground black pepper. Add the fish, toss to coat well, and leave to marinate for 20 minutes.

Heat the oil in a saucepan or wok, then add the onions, chilies, and curry paste. Stirring occasionally, cook over low heat for 10 minutes or until fragrant. Add the fish and shrimp, and stir to coat in the curry paste mixture. Cook for 3 minutes or until the shrimp just turn pink, then add the squid and cook for 1 minute.

Add the stock and bring to a boil, then reduce the heat and simmer for 2 minutes or until the seafood is cooked and tender. Season to taste with salt and freshly ground black pepper. Top with the shredded basil leaves.

malaysian nonya chicken curry . . . . serves 4

IN THE FIFTEENTH CENTURY, THE STRAIT OF MALACCA WAS THE FAVORED ROUTE OF CHINESE TRADERS TO ARABIA AND INDIA. MANY SETTLED IN THE AREA AND MARRIED THE LOCAL WOMEN, WHO BECAME KNOWN AS NONYA. A UNIQUE CUISINE DEVELOPED, WHICH BLENDED CHINESE TECHNIQUES AND MALAYSIAN SPICES.

curry paste

shrimp paste	1/2 teaspoon
red onions	2, chopped
red chilies	4, seeded
garlic	4 cloves, crushed
lemongrass	2 stems, white part only, sliced
galangal	1 1/4-inch cube, sliced
Kaffir lime leaves	8, roughly chopped
ground turmeric	1 teaspoon
oil	2 tablespoons
boneless, skinless chicken thighs	1 pound 10 ounces, cut into bite-size pieces
unsweetened coconut milk	14 fluid-ounce can, or 1 2/3 cups
tamarind puree	3 1/2 tablespoons
fish sauce	1 tablespoon
Kaffir lime leaves	3, shredded

Dry-fry the shrimp paste wrapped in some foil in a frying pan over medium-high heat for 2–3 minutes or until fragrant. Allow to cool.

Combine the shrimp paste with the remaining curry paste ingredients in a food processor or in a mortar with a pestle. Process or pound to a smooth paste.

Heat a wok or large saucepan over high heat, add the oil, and swirl to coat. Add the curry paste and cook, stirring occasionally, over low heat for 8–10 minutes or until fragrant. Add the chicken and stir-fry with the paste for 2–3 minutes.

Add the coconut milk, tamarind puree, and fish sauce to the wok. Stirring occasionally, simmer for 15–20 minutes or until the chicken is tender. Garnish with the shredded lime leaves.

Put the paste ingredients in a food processor or mortar.

Process or pound the mixture until a smooth paste is formed.

goan fish curry

GOA IS SITUATED ON INDIA'S SOUTHWEST COAST, WHERE SEAFOOD IS A STAPLE INGREDIENT. THE OTHER FAVORITE INGREDIENT IS COCONUT, AND FEW DISHES ARE WITHOUT IT. DISHES, INCLUDING THIS ONE, ARE TYPICALLY RICH, SIMPLE, AND PLEASANTLY SPICY WITH CHILIES, GINGER, TURMERIC, AND TAMARIND.

oil	3 tablespoons
onion	1 large, finely chopped
garlic	4–5 cloves, crushed
ginger	2 teaspoons grated
dried red chilies	4–6
coriander seeds	1 tablespoon
cumin seeds	2 teaspoons
ground turmeric	1 teaspoon
chili powder	1/4 teaspoon
dried coconut	1/3 cup
unsweetened coconut milk	1 cup
tomatoes	2, peeled and chopped
tamarind puree	2 tablespoons
white vinegar	1 tablespoon
curry leaves	6
skinless, firm white fish fillets	2 pounds 4 ounces, cut into 3-inch pieces

Heat the oil in a large saucepan. Add the onion and cook, stirring, over low heat for 10 minutes or until softened and lightly golden. Add the garlic and ginger, and cook for an additional 2 minutes.

Dry-fry the dried chilies, coriander seeds, cumin seeds, turmeric, chili powder, and coconut in a frying pan over medium-high heat for 2–3 minutes or until fragrant. Allow to cool. Using a mortar with a pestle or a spice grinder, crush or grind to a powder.

Add the spice mixture, coconut milk, tomatoes, tamarind, vinegar, and curry leaves to the onion mixture. Stir to mix thoroughly, add 1 cup water, and simmer, stirring frequently, for 10 minutes or until the tomatoes soften and the mixture thickens slightly.

Add the fish and cook covered over low heat for 10 minutes or until cooked through. Stir gently once or twice during cooking and add a little water if the mixture is too thick.

Dry-fry the spices and dried coconut until aromatic.

Use a mortar with a pestle or spice grinder to grind the spices.

Stir the coconut milk into the onion and spice mixture.

three ways with yogurt

FOR DINERS EATING A FIERY CURRY, YOGURT IS OFTEN A GREAT SAVIOR. IT IS USED IN NUMEROUS SIDE DISHES, SPECIFICALLY DESIGNED TO ACCOMPANY SPICY MEALS, OF WHICH PERHAPS THE MOST FAMOUS EXAMPLES ARE INDIAN RAITAS. THESE FRESH, SIMPLE YOGURT PREPARATIONS CAN BE MIXED WITH GRATED VEGETABLES, HERBS, SPICES, OR COCONUT—WHATEVER SUITS THE CURRY. EQUALLY CREAMY AND SOOTHING ARE CHURRIS, WHICH ALSO CONTAIN BUTTERMILK, AND CARROT PACHADI, A SLIGHTLY SPICIER BLEND.

churri (yogurt and buttermilk side dish)

Dry-fry 1 teaspoon cumin seeds in a frying pan over medium-high heat for 2–3 minutes or until fragrant. Allow to cool. Using a mortar with a pestle or a spice grinder, crush or grind to a powder. Roughly chop 1 large handful mint leaves and cilantro leaves. Put the mint and cilantro in a food processor with a 3/4-inch piece ginger and 2 green chilies and process to a smooth paste. Add 1 1/4 cups Greek-style yogurt (or plain yogurt drained in cheesecloth), 1 1/4 cups buttermilk, and a pinch of salt to the mixture. Process until all the ingredients are well mixed. Season, then mix in 1 thinly sliced onion and the ground cumin, reserving a little cumin to sprinkle over the top. Serves 4.

cucumber and tomato raita

Put 2 1/4 cups grated cucumber and 1 large, finely chopped ripe tomato in a strainer for 20 minutes to drain off any excess liquid. Mix them in a bowl with 1 1/4 cups Greek-style yogurt (or plain yogurt drained in cheesecloth), and season with salt. Heat 1/2 tablespoon oil in a small saucepan over medium heat, and add 1 teaspoon black mustard seeds. Then cover and shake the pan until the seeds start to pop. Pour the seeds and oil over the yogurt. Serve garnished with chopped cilantro leaves. Serves 4.

carrot pachadi (yogurt and carrot side dish)

Heat 1 tablespoon oil in a small saucepan over medium heat. Add 1 teaspoon black mustard seeds and 2–3 dried chilies. Then cover and shake the pan until the seeds start to pop. Remove from the heat and immediately stir in a pinch of asafetida and 1 stalk of curry leaves. Put 2 1/3 cups Greek-style yogurt (or plain yogurt drained in cheesecloth) in a bowl and whisk to remove any lumps. Mix in 4 grated carrots, the mustard seeds, chilies, asafetida, and curry leaves along with the oil. Season with salt. Garnish with cilantro leaves. Serves 4.

beef balls with pickled garlic

serves 4

THIS DISH INVOLVES LITTLE PREPARATION, MAKING IT A WELCOME CHOICE WHEN YOU FEEL LIKE A CURRY BUT CAN'T BE BOTHERED WITH THE GRINDING AND ROASTING. PICKLED GARLIC HAS A SWEET–SOUR FLAVOR AND IS USED IN CURRIES AS A MEANS OF BALANCING OTHER FLAVORS—BE THEY HOT, CREAMY, OR SWEET.

meatballs

ground beef	1 pound
garlic	3 cloves, crushed
white pepper	1 teaspoon
cilantro	1 small handful leaves, chopped
Thai basil leaves	1 small handful, chopped
scallion	1, finely chopped
fish sauce	3 teaspoons
egg	1
oil	3 tablespoons
green curry paste	3 tablespoons, store-bought or see recipe on page 130
ginger	3 tablespoons finely chopped
ground turmeric	1 1/2 teaspoons
fish sauce	3 tablespoons
Kaffir lime leaves	3
tamarind puree	2 1/2 tablespoons
pickled garlic	3 tablespoons chopped
jaggery	1 1/2 tablespoons shaved (or 1 1/2 tablespoons brown sugar)

To make the meatballs, combine all the ingredients together well. Roll a tablespoon at a time of the mixture into small balls. This should make about 24 balls.

Heat the oil in a heavy-based saucepan over medium heat and add the curry paste, ginger, and turmeric. Stirring frequently, cook for about 5 minutes or until fragrant.

Add the fish sauce, lime leaves, and tamarind. Bring to a boil, then cover. Reduce to a simmer and cook for 5 minutes. Add the meatballs, pickled garlic, and jaggery, and simmer for 15 minutes or until the meatballs are cooked through.

Roll tablespoons of the beef mixture into 24 balls.

Add the meatballs to the sauce and simmer until cooked through.

malaysian hot and sour pineapple curry

. . . . serves 6

PINEAPPLE ADDS A TOUCH OF TART SWEETNESS TO CURRIES AND IS POPULAR IN VEGETARIAN MEALS. HERE, IT IS MIXED WITH HOT CHILIES, CREAMY COCONUT, AND THE MELLOW WARMTH OF CLOVES AND CINNAMON TO PRODUCE A REFRESHING DISH THAT IS A LITTLE BIT SWEET AND A LITTLE BIT SPICY.

pineapple	1 semiripe, cored, cut into chunks
ground turmeric	1/2 teaspoon
star anise	1
cinnamon stick	1, broken into small pieces
cloves	7
cardamom pods	7, bruised
oil	1 tablespoon
onion	1, finely chopped
ginger	1 teaspoon grated
garlic	1 clove, crushed
red chilies	5, chopped
sugar	1 tablespoon
unsweetened coconut cream	3 tablespoons

Put the pineapple in a saucepan, cover with water, and add the turmeric. Put the star anise, cinnamon, cloves, and cardamom pods on a square of cheesecloth, and tie securely with string. Add the spice bag to the pan and cook over medium heat for 10 minutes. Squeeze the bag to extract any flavor, then discard. Reserve the cooking liquid.

Heat the oil in a frying pan, add the onion, ginger, garlic, and chilies. Stirring, cook for 1–2 minutes or until fragrant. Add the pineapple, the cooking liquid, and sugar. Salt to taste. Cook for 2 minutes, then stir in the coconut cream. Cook, stirring, over low heat for 3–5 minutes or until the sauce thickens. Serve this curry hot or cold.

A native of tropical South America, the pineapple is actually several individual fruits joined together: each of these fruits are the result of numerous unfertilized flowers that have fused. To most of us, however, it is a deliciously juicy and sweet fruit, the very emblem of warm weather. Like most fruit, pineapple is best eaten fresh, but it is also used in dishes such as curries, ice creams, sorbets, and cakes. Pineapples do not continue to ripen after being picked, so choose well. Select pineapples that are heavy for their size and sweetly aromatic.

tamarind fish curry .... serves 4

TAMARIND IS WIDELY USED IN INDIAN AND SOUTHEAST ASIAN COOKING FOR ITS SWEET–SOUR FLAVOR AND SOURING PROPERTIES. HERE, THE TAMARIND IS BALANCED BY FULL-BODIED PEPPERCORNS, CUMIN, AND CORIANDER; MADE AROMATIC WITH PUNGENT SAFFRON AND SWEET CARDAMOM; AND CREAMY WITH THICK YOGURT.

skinless, firm white fish fillets	1 pound 5 ounces
ground turmeric	1 teaspoon
powdered saffron	pinch
garlic	3 cloves, crushed
lemon juice	2 teaspoons
cumin seeds	1 teaspoon
coriander seeds	2 tablespoons
white peppercorns	1 teaspoon
cardamom pods	4, bruised
ginger	2 1/2 tablespoons finely chopped
red chilies	2, thinly sliced
oil	2 tablespoons
onion	1, chopped
red bell pepper	1, cut into 3/4-inch squares
green bell pepper	1, cut into 3/4-inch squares
plum tomatoes	4, diced
tamarind puree	2 tablespoons
plain yogurt	3/4 cup
cilantro	2 tablespoons chopped leaves

Rinse the fish fillets and pat dry. Prick the fillets with a fork. Combine the turmeric, saffron, garlic, lemon juice, and 1 teaspoon salt. Rub this mixture over the fish fillets. Refrigerate for 2–3 hours.

Dry-fry the cumin seeds, coriander seeds, peppercorns, and cardamom in a frying pan over medium-high heat for 2–3 minutes or until fragrant. Allow to cool. Using a mortar with a pestle or a spice grinder, crush or grind to a powder. Combine with the ginger and chilies.

Heat the oil in a heavy-based saucepan over medium heat and add the onion, red and green bell peppers, and ground spice mix. Cook gently for 10 minutes or until aromatic and the onion is transparent. Increase the heat to high, add the tomatoes, 1 cup water, and the tamarind. Bring to a boil, then reduce to a simmer and cook for 20 minutes.

Rinse the paste off the fish and chop into 1 1/4-inch pieces. Add to the pan and continue to simmer for 10 minutes. Stir in the yogurt and chopped cilantro and serve.

Rub the saffron mixture into the fish fillets and leave for 2–3 hours.

Dry-fry the spices until aromatic, then grind to a fine powder.

Add the onion, bell peppers, and spice mix to the saucepan.

pork and bitter melon curry...................................... serves 4

THIS IS AN IMPRESSIVE LOOKING CURRY, WITH ITS STUFFED BITTER MELON COMMANDING ATTENTION. IN THIS DISH, THIS DISTINCTIVE VEGETABLE IS BALANCED BY OTHER STRONG FLAVORS, INCLUDING PORK, GARLIC, AND CHILIES. DESPITE ITS NAME, BITTER MELON IS ACTUALLY QUITE DELICIOUS.

bitter melon	6 medium
	(about 25 ounces in total)
sugar	2 tablespoons

pork filling

ground pork	9 ounces
ginger	1 teaspoon chopped
white peppercorns	1/2 teaspoon, crushed
garlic	1 clove, crushed
scallion	1, finely chopped
paprika	1 teaspoon
water chestnuts	2 tablespoons finely chopped
Kaffir lime leaves	2, thinly sliced
crushed peanuts	1 1/2 tablespoons
cilantro	1 small handful leaves, chopped
jaggery	1 tablespoon shaved
	(or 1 tablespoon brown sugar)
fish sauce	1 tablespoon

oil	3 tablespoons
red curry paste	2 tablespoons, store-bought or
	see recipe on page 18
jaggery	1 tablespoon shaved
	(or 1 tablespoon brown sugar)
fish sauce	2 tablespoons
unsweetened coconut cream	1 cup
Kaffir lime leaves	4

Discard the ends of the bitter melon, then cut into 1-inch slices. Hollow out the fibrous center membrane and seeds with a small knife, leaving the outside rings intact. Bring 3 cups water to a boil with the sugar and 3 teaspoons salt. Blanch the melon for 2 minutes and drain.

Combine all the ingredients for the pork filling. Pack this into the melon pieces. Heat 2 tablespoons of the oil in a heavy-based saucepan over low heat. Add the melon and cook for 3 minutes on each side or until the pork is golden and sealed. Set the pieces aside.

Heat the remaining oil in the pan and add the red curry paste. Stir for 3 minutes or until aromatic. Add the jaggery and fish sauce, and stir until the jaggery dissolves. Add the coconut cream, 1 cup water, and the lime leaves. Simmer for 5 minutes, then carefully add the bitter melon. Continue simmering for 20 minutes or until the pork is cooked and the melon is tender, turning the pieces halfway through cooking.

Note: English cucumbers can be used instead of bitter melon. Follow the same method above.

Cut the bitter melon into slices and hollow out the center.

Pack the pork filling into the bitter melon slices.

hot and sour
eggplant curry

.... serves 4

EGGPLANT GOES PARTICULARLY WELL WITH CORIANDER, CUMIN, AND COCONUT—RICH, WARM FLAVORS—BUT IS SURPRISINGLY AMENABLE TO A WIDE RANGE OF INGREDIENTS, SUCH AS THE CURRY-SCENTED FENUGREEK AND ANISE-FLAVORED FENNEL USED IN THIS DISH.

eggplant	1 large
tomatoes	2 small
oil	2 tablespoons
fenugreek seeds	3 teaspoons
fennel seeds	3 teaspoons
garlic	4 cloves, crushed
onion	1 large, finely diced
curry leaves	4
ground coriander	1 1/2 tablespoons
ground turmeric	2 teaspoons
tomato juice	1/2 cup
tamarind puree	2 tablespoons
red chilies	2, thinly sliced
unsweetened coconut cream	1/2 cup
cilantro	1 handful leaves, chopped

Cut the eggplant into 3/4-inch cubes. Sprinkle with 1/2 teaspoon salt and set aside for 1 hour. Drain and rinse.

Roughly dice the tomatoes and set aside. Heat the oil in a heavy-based saucepan over medium heat. Add the fenugreek and fennel seeds. When they start to crackle, add the garlic, onion, and curry leaves, and cook for 3–5 minutes or until the onion is transparent. Add the eggplant and stir for 6 minutes or until it begins to soften. Add the tomatoes, ground spices, tomato juice, tamarind, and chili.

Bring to a boil, then reduce to a simmer. Cover and continue to cook for about 35 minutes or until the eggplant is very soft. Stir in the coconut cream and cilantro, and season to taste.

Roughly dice the tomatoes, keeping the skin and seeds.

Cook the onion for 3–5 minutes or until it becomes transparent.

When the eggplant is very soft, stir in the coconut cream.

the perfect rice

Anywhere there is curry, rice will be close by. Although three basic rice types are available, only long-grained is considered the natural accompaniment to curries. Compared with short- and medium-grained rices, long-grained is generally thinner, longer, less starchy, and yields a light, fluffy, loose-grained texture when cooked. Although several varieties of long-grained rice are available, any will do the trick in a pinch. For authenticity, try serving the dry, separate-grained, nutty-tasting basmati rice with Indian curries, and the aromatic, slightly clingy, floral-scented jasmine rice alongside Thai curries. The flavors of both these rice varieties complement the spices in the curries from the corresponding cuisines.

Absorption method

Put the rice in a saucepan and shake so that it evenly coats the bottom of the pan. Stick the very tip of your finger into the rice, then add enough cold water to come up to the first finger joint. Bring to a boil over high heat, then cover with a clear, tight-fitting lid. Reduce the heat to low and cook until the water mostly evaporates and small steam holes appear on the surface of the rice. Remove the lid, fluff the grains with a fork, and serve.

Rapid-boil method

Bring a large saucepan of water to a boil over high heat. Sprinkle over the rice and cook according to the instructions on the package, or until the grains are tender. Drain the rice in a colander. If using jasmine rice, which is slightly glutinous, rinse with a little lukewarm water before serving.

balti-style lamb .... serves 4

BALTISTAN MAY SIT HIGH IN THE MOUNTAINS OF NORTH PAKISTAN, BUT BIRMINGHAM, ENGLAND, HAS BECOME THE INTERNATIONAL LAUNCH PAD OF BALTI CUISINE. DISTINCTIVE FOR ITS USE OF THE TWO-HANDLED *KARAHI* POT, IT ALSO FEATURES ITS OWN MASALA PASTE, WHICH IS HERBY AND FRAGRANT WITH GREEN CARDAMOM.

lamb leg steaks	2 pounds 4 ounces, cut into 1 1/4-inch cubes
ready-made Balti masala paste	5 tablespoons (see note)
ghee or oil	2 tablespoons
garlic	3 cloves, crushed
garam masala	1 tablespoon
onion	1 large, finely chopped
cilantro	2 tablespoons chopped leaves, plus extra for garnish

Preheat the oven to 375°F. Combine the lamb, 1 tablespoon of the Balti masala paste, and 1 1/2 cups boiling water in a large casserole dish or karahi. Cook covered in the oven for 30–40 minutes or until the meat is almost cooked through. Drain, reserving the stock.

Heat the ghee or oil in a wok, add the garlic and garam masala, and stir-fry over medium heat for 1 minute. Add the onion and cook for 5–7 minutes or until the onion is soft and golden brown. Increase the heat, and add the remaining masala paste and the lamb to the wok. Cook for 5 minutes to brown the meat. Slowly add the reserved stock and simmer over low heat, stirring occasionally, for 15 minutes.

Add the chopped cilantro leaves and 3/4 cup water, and simmer for 15 minutes or until the lamb is tender and the sauce thickens slightly. Season with salt and freshly ground black pepper and garnish with extra cilantro leaves.

Note: Balti masala paste is available at Asian food stores.

Ghee is most often associated with Indian cooking, but its usefulness as a cooking medium means it is now used throughout Southeast Asia. It is a clarified butter—that is, butter that has been melted and boiled to remove milk solids and water. The resulting ghee has a high burning point, little moisture, and a high fat content, so a little goes a long way. Most importantly, ghee has a strong nutty flavor and rich, toasted aroma, which is used to advantage in meat and vegetable curries, lentil dals, and rice dishes. Buy from Asian and Indian food stores and store in a cool, dark place.

duck and coconut curry........................serves 6

THE USE OF SOUR VINEGAR IN A CURRY MAY SEEM AN UNUSUAL ADDITION, BUT IT CAN PROVIDE AN EXCELLENT FOIL FOR RICH COCONUT MILK AND FATTY MEAT SUCH AS DUCK. IN INDIA, IT IS OFTEN FOUND IN REGIONAL COOKING THAT HAS BEEN INFLUENCED BY OTHER CULTURES, SUCH AS THE FOOD OF GOA AND THE PARSIS.

curry paste

coriander seeds	1 1/2 teaspoons
cardamom seeds	1 teaspoon
fenugreek seeds	1 teaspoon
brown mustard seeds	1 teaspoon
black peppercorns	10
red onion	1, chopped
garlic	2 cloves, crushed
red chilies	4, seeded, chopped
cilantro	2 roots, chopped
ginger	2 teaspoons grated
garam masala	2 teaspoons
ground turmeric	1/4 teaspoon
tamarind puree	2 teaspoons
duck breast fillets	6
red onion	1, sliced
white vinegar	1/2 cup
unsweetened coconut milk	2 cups
cilantro	1 small handful leaves

Dry-fry the coriander, cardamom, fenugreek, and mustard seeds in a frying pan over medium-high heat for 2–3 minutes or until fragrant. Allow to cool. Using a mortar with a pestle or a spice grinder, crush or grind the spices with the black peppercorns to a powder.

Combine the ground spices with the remaining curry paste ingredients in a food processor or in a mortar with a pestle. Process or pound to a smooth paste.

Trim any excess fat from the duck, then place skin-side down in a large saucepan and cook over medium heat for 10 minutes or until the skin is brown and any remaining fat melts. Turn the duck over and cook for 5 minutes or until tender. Remove and drain on paper towels.

Reserve 1 tablespoon duck fat and discard the remaining fat. Add the onion and cook for 5 minutes, then add the curry paste and stir over low heat for 10 minutes or until fragrant.

Return the duck to the pan and stir to coat with the paste. Stir in the vinegar, coconut milk, 1 teaspoon salt, and 1/2 cup water. Simmer covered for 45 minutes or until the duck is tender. Stir in the cilantro leaves just before serving.

Process the onion, garlic, spices, and tamarind until smooth.

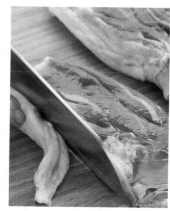

Trim the excess fat from the duck before adding to the pan.

sour lamb and bamboo curry .... serves 4

BAMBOO SHOOTS ARE USED MAINLY IN SOUTHEAST ASIAN COOKING. WHEN FRESH, THEY HAVE A LOVELY CRISP, NUTTY BITTERNESS TO THEM. THEY ARE AVAILABLE IN ASIAN FOOD STORES, BUT THE CANNED VARIETY MAKES AN ACCEPTABLE SUBSTITUTE. ALONG WITH THE GREEN BEANS AND LAMB, THEY PROVIDE TEXTURE TO THIS CURRY.

curry paste

white peppercorns	1 teaspoon
shrimp paste	1 teaspoon
dried shrimp	1/2 cup
scallions	6, sliced
jalapeño chilies	1/3 cup sliced, in brine
lemongrass	2 stems, white part only, thinly sliced
garlic	6 cloves, crushed
cilantro	4 roots, chopped
ground galangal	2 teaspoons
chili powder	1 teaspoon
fish sauce	1/3 cup
lime juice	1/3 cup
ground turmeric	1 teaspoon
boneless lamb leg	1 pound 2 ounces, trimmed of excess fat
oil	1 tablespoon
jaggery	1 tablespoon shaved (or 1 tablespoon brown sugar)
unsweetened coconut cream	1 cup
tamarind puree	1/4 cup
fish sauce	1 1/2 tablespoons
bamboo shoot pieces	3 cups, canned, cut into thick wedges
green beans	1 1/2 cups cut into 1 1/2-inch lengths

In a frying pan over medium-high heat, dry-fry the peppercorns and the shrimp paste wrapped in some foil for 2–3 minutes or until fragrant. Allow to cool. Using a mortar with a pestle or a spice grinder, crush or grind the peppercorns to a powder. Process the dried shrimp in a food processor until it becomes very finely shredded—forming a "floss."

Combine the crushed peppercorns and the shrimp with the remaining curry paste ingredients in a food processor or in a mortar with a pestle. Process or pound to a smooth paste.

Slice the lamb into 2 x 3/4-inch strips, about 1/8-inch thick. Heat the oil in a flameproof casserole dish over medium heat. Add 2–3 tablespoons of the paste, stirring constantly. Then add the jaggery and stir until dissolved. Add the lamb to the dish, stirring for 7 minutes or until lightly golden.

Add the coconut cream, 1 cup water, tamarind, fish sauce, and bamboo shoots. Bring to a boil, then reduce the heat and simmer for about 20 minutes or until tender. Add the beans and simmer for another 3 minutes. Season to taste and serve.

thai hot and sour
shrimp and winter squash curry .... serves 4

FLAVORED WITH RED CURRY PASTE, PERFUMED BY KAFFIR LIME LEAVES, AND SEASONED WITH TAMARIND, FISH SAUCE, LIME JUICE, AND CHILIES, THIS DELICIOUS CURRY IS A REAL MEAL-IN-A-BOWL. THE FLAVORS ARE WELL BALANCED, WITH A BIT OF BITE AND A LOVELY TANGY TASTE, AND DO NOT OVERPOWER THE SHRIMP.

Lebanese (short) cucumber	1
unsweetened coconut cream	14 fluid-ounce can (do not shake the can)
red curry paste	1½ tablespoons, store-bought or see recipe on page 18
fish sauce	3 tablespoons
jaggery	2 tablespoons shaved (or 2 tablespoons brown sugar)
winter squash	1¾ cups, cut into ¾-inch cubes
straw mushrooms	14-ounce can, drained
raw shrimp	1 pound 2 ounces, peeled, deveined, tails intact
tamarind puree	2 tablespoons
red chilies	2, chopped
lime juice	1 tablespoon
Kaffir lime leaves	4
cilantro	4 roots, chopped
bean sprouts	1 small handful, to serve
cilantro	1 small handful leaves, to serve

Peel and cut the cucumber in half lengthwise, then scrape out the seeds with a teaspoon and thinly slice.

Put the thick coconut cream from the top of the can in a saucepan, bring to a rapid simmer over medium heat, stirring occasionally, and cook for 5–10 minutes or until the mixture "splits" (the oil starts to separate). Add the red curry paste and stir for 2–3 minutes or until fragrant. Add the fish sauce and jaggery and stir until the jaggery dissolves.

Add the remaining coconut cream, squash, and 3 tablespoons of water. Cover and bring to a boil. Reduce to a simmer and cook for 10 minutes or until the squash is just starting to become tender. Add the cucumber, straw mushrooms, shrimp, tamarind, chilies, lime juice, lime leaves, and cilantro roots. Cover, increase the heat, and bring to a boil again. Then reduce to a simmer and cook for 3–5 minutes or until the shrimp are just cooked through. Garnish with bean sprouts and cilantro leaves.

It's hard to believe chilies aren't indigenous to Asia, such is their importance in cuisines stretching from India to Indonesia. However, since their introduction to the region in the sixteenth century, they have become inextricably linked with the local diets. Thousands of varieties of chili plants grow, with pods in an assortment of shapes, sizes, and colors, and varying in their degree of hotness from gentle to positively painful. But chilies are not merely hot; each has its own flavor. Dried and fresh chilies also taste very different. Some popular varieties used in curries include cayenne, kashmiri, and bird's-eye chilies.

aromatic

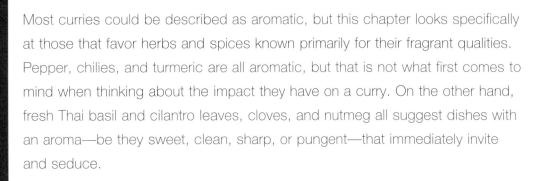

Most curries could be described as aromatic, but this chapter looks specifically at those that favor herbs and spices known primarily for their fragrant qualities. Pepper, chilies, and turmeric are all aromatic, but that is not what first comes to mind when thinking about the impact they have on a curry. On the other hand, fresh Thai basil and cilantro leaves, cloves, and nutmeg all suggest dishes with an aroma—be they sweet, clean, sharp, or pungent—that immediately invite and seduce.

Thai cooking in particular makes good use of fresh herbs to engage the sense of smell. If Indian cooking excels at combining dried spices, Thai cooking delights in creating curries with layers of flavor and aroma from a wide range of fresh herbs, spices, and seasonings. These include local ingredients such as the aniseedlike Thai basil, floral Kaffir lime leaves, and tangy galangal, as well as more familiar ones such as cilantro, ginger, lemongrass, garlic, scallions, and onions. It is sometimes easy to overlook the importance of these reliable stalwarts, but few curries could do without the body and flavor they provide, as well as their sharp, clean, and sweet aromas.

A Thai green curry is the classic example of this art, blending such ingredients with chicken, vegetables, or fish in a coconut-based sauce, with green chilies for heat. The finished dish—tart, salty, and hot—is generously garnished with fresh-tasting, fragrant Kaffir lime and Thai basil leaves. Thai curries are renowned for the care taken in preparing and cooking these ingredients; frying curry paste is a careful exercise in letting your nose tell you when to add the next ingredient. Learning to recognize the different aromas of herbs and spices is not essential for the occasional curry cook—you'll still produce delicious results—but is certainly something to which dedicated lovers of curries aspire.

Apart from a number of Thai curries, this chapter also features various Indian curries, including spicy and fragrant fish *koftas* and a lamb and spinach curry whose heady blend of cumin, coriander seeds, black peppercorns, Indian bay (cassia) leaves, garam masala, turmeric, and paprika is classically Indian and extremely inviting. Finally, this chapter also features a *dum aloo*, which is based on a traditional method of steaming ingredients in their own juices and flavorings. Fragrant with cardamom, cloves, cinnamon, ginger, cumin, and chilies, the aromas will tempt you long before the dish is on the table.

spiced chicken with almonds .... serves 6

THIS IS A WONDERFULLY SIMPLE AND AROMATIC DISH, WITH LITTLE OF THE SHARPNESS OR SPICINESS FOUND IN MANY CURRIES. THE MOGUL EMPERORS FIRST INTRODUCED ALMONDS TO INDIA WHERE THEY REMAIN ASSOCIATED WITH SUMPTUOUS DINING. IN THIS DISH, THEY ARE USED BOTH IN THE SAUCE AND AS A GARNISH.

oil	3 tablespoons
slivered almonds	1/4 cup
red onions	2, finely chopped
garlic	4–6 cloves, crushed
ginger	1 tablespoon grated
cardamom pods	4, bruised
cloves	4
ground cumin	1 teaspoon
ground coriander	1 teaspoon
ground turmeric	1 teaspoon
chili powder	1/2 teaspoon
boneless, skinless chicken thighs	2 pounds 4 ounces, trimmed
tomatoes	2 large, peeled, chopped
cinnamon stick	1
ground almonds	1 cup

Heat 1 tablespoon of the oil in a large saucepan. Add the almonds and cook over low heat for 15 seconds or until lightly golden brown. Remove and drain on crumpled paper towels.

Heat the remaining oil and add the onion. Stirring, cook for 8 minutes or until golden brown. Add the garlic and ginger, and cook, stirring, for 2 minutes. Then stir in the spices. Reduce the heat to low and cook for 2 minutes or until aromatic.

Add the chicken and cook, stirring constantly, for 5 minutes or until well coated and the spices start to brown.

Stir in the tomatoes, cinnamon stick, ground almonds, and 1 cup hot water. Simmer covered over low heat for 1 hour or until the chicken is cooked through and tender. Stir often and add a little more water, if needed.

Let sit covered for 30 minutes to allow the flavors to develop. Remove the cinnamon stick, sprinkle with the almonds, and serve.

Cook the almonds until golden, then drain on paper towels.

Toss the chicken pieces in the spices, coating well.

Add the tomatoes, cinnamon, and ground almonds. Simmer.

creamy shrimp curry .... serves 4

CREAMY, YES, BUT ALSO FRAGRANT WITH CLOVES, CARDAMOM, CINNAMON, AND INDIAN BAY LEAVES. MAKE SURE YOU USE INDIAN BAY LEAVES AND NOT THE EUROPEAN VARIETY. THEY SHOULD MORE ACCURATELY BE CALLED CASSIA LEAVES, AS THEY ARE FROM THAT TREE. THEY ARE SPICY AND REFRESHING, WITH A SWEET, WOODY AROMA.

tiger shrimp	1 pound 2 ounces, peeled, deveined, with tails intact
lemon juice	1 1/2 tablespoons
oil	3 tablespoons
onion	1/2, finely chopped
ground turmeric	1/2 teaspoon
cinnamon stick	1
cloves	4
cardamom pods	7, bruised
Indian bay (cassia) leaves	5
ginger	3/4-inch piece, grated
garlic	3 cloves, crushed
chili powder	1 teaspoon
unsweetened coconut milk	2/3 cup

Put the shrimp in a bowl, add the lemon juice, toss together, and set aside for 5 minutes. Rinse the shrimp under running cold water and pat dry with paper towels.

Heat the oil in a heavy-based frying pan and fry the onion until lightly browned. Add the turmeric, cinnamon, cloves, cardamom, bay leaves, ginger, and garlic. Fry for 1 minute. Add the chili powder, coconut milk, season with salt, and slowly bring to a boil. Reduce the heat and simmer for 2 minutes.

Add the shrimp and return to a boil. Reduce the heat and simmer for 5 minutes or until the shrimp are cooked through and the sauce is thick.

Add the spices to the browned onion and cook until fragrant.

Simmer the shrimp gently until just curled and cooked through.

pork and cardamom curry .... serves 6

TENDER, SWEET PORK FILLET IS PERFECT FOR THIS DISH: IT IS FAT FREE, SO IT NEEDS AN INITIAL BRIEF COOKING TO SEAL IN THE JUICES, BUT THEN IT WILL COOK FAIRLY QUICKLY IN THE CURRY. THE SPICES—PEPPERCORNS, GINGER, CARDAMOM, CUMIN, GARAM MASALA—COMBINE TO GIVE THIS DISH A LOVELY WARM, EXOTIC FLAVOR.

curry paste

cardamom pods	10
ginger	2½-inch piece, chopped
garlic	3 cloves, crushed
black peppercorns	2 teaspoons
cinnamon stick	1
onion	1, thinly sliced
ground cumin	1 teaspoon
ground coriander	1 teaspoon
garam masala	1 teaspoon
oil	3 tablespoons
pork fillet	2 pounds 4 ounces, thinly sliced
tomatoes	2, finely diced
chicken stock	½ cup
unsweetened coconut milk	½ cup

Lightly crush the cardamom pods with the flat side of a heavy knife. Remove the seeds and discard the pods. Put the seeds and the remaining curry paste ingredients in a food processor or in a mortar with a pestle. Process or pound to a smooth paste.

Put 2½ tablespoons of the oil in a large, heavy-based frying pan, and fry the pork in batches until browned. Set aside. Add the remaining oil and the curry paste to the pan. Cook over medium-high heat for 3–4 minutes or until aromatic. Add the tomatoes, stock, and coconut milk. Simmer covered over low-medium heat for 15 minutes. While cooking, skim and discard any oil that surfaces.

Add the pork to the sauce and simmer uncovered for 5 minutes or until cooked. Season well to taste and serve.

Warm and pungent, with lemony undertones, cardamom has been chewed as a breath freshener from the time of the ancient Egyptians to today. Many varieties of cardamom are grown, but the smooth green pods from their native southern India and Sri Lanka are considered the best. Also of note are the large, wrinkled black (brown) pods, which have a coarser flavor. Green cardamom is difficult to harvest, making it expensive and highly valued. It is used in both sweet and savory Indian and Asian dishes, and both black and green cardamom are essential components of garam masala. Green cardamom is sometimes bleached to form white cardamom.

dum aloo...serves 6

IN INDIA, *DUM* MEANS TO COOK BY STEAMING——IT TRANSLATES AS "TO BREATHE IN." TRADITIONALLY, A POT WAS FILLED WITH INGREDIENTS, THE LID SEALED WITH DOUGH, AND THE POT SET OVER COALS. THE FOOD COOKED SLOWLY AND DELICATELY IN ITS OWN STEAM AND JUICES.

curry paste

cardamom pods	4
ginger	1 teaspoon grated
garlic	2 cloves, crushed
red chilies	3
cumin seeds	1 teaspoon
cashews	1/4 cup
white poppy seeds	1 tablespoon
cinnamon stick	1
cloves	6
all-purpose potatoes	6, cubed
onions	2, roughly chopped
oil	2 tablespoons
ground turmeric	1/2 teaspoon
chickpea flour	1 teaspoon
plain yogurt	1 cup
cilantro	leaves, to garnish

Lightly crush the cardamom pods with the flat side of a heavy knife. Remove the seeds and discard the pods. Put the seeds and the remaining curry paste ingredients in a food processor or in a mortar with a pestle. Process or pound into a smooth paste.

Bring a large saucepan of lightly salted water to a boil. Add the potatoes and cook for 5–6 minutes or until just tender, then drain.

Put the onion in a food processor and process in short bursts until it is finely chopped but not pureed. Heat the oil in a large saucepan, add the onion, and cook over low heat for 5 minutes. Add the curry paste and cook, stirring, for another 5 minutes or until fragrant. Stir in the potatoes, turmeric, and 1 cup water. Season with salt.

Reduce the heat and simmer, tightly covered, for 10 minutes or until the potatoes are cooked but not breaking up, and the sauce thickens slightly.

Combine the chickpea flour with the yogurt and add to the potato mixture. Stirring, cook over low heat for 5 minutes or until thickened again. Garnish with the cilantro leaves and serve.

Lightly crush the cardamom pods to release the seeds.

Pulse the onions in a food processor until finely chopped.

Stir in the yogurt mixture and cook until thickened.

indonesian chicken in coconut milk . . . . serves 6

THIS HEADY DISH PERFECTLY CONJURES UP INDONESIA'S TROPICAL CLIMATE AND PRODUCE. CURRIES ARE TYPICALLY RICH, RELYING ON INGREDIENTS SUCH AS PEPPER, GALANGAL, CORIANDER, AND SHRIMP PASTE FOR HOT, TANGY, AND SALTY ELEMENTS. NUTMEG, THOUGH NATIVE TO THE AREA, IS A SURPRISINGLY RARE CURRY ADDITION.

curry paste

shrimp paste	1/2 teaspoon
coriander seeds	2 teaspoons
cumin seeds	1/2 teaspoon
white peppercorns	2 teaspoons
lemongrass	2 stems, white part only, sliced
red onions	2, chopped
garlic	3 cloves, crushed
ginger	1 tablespoon grated
galangal	2 1/2 tablespoons grated
ground nutmeg	1/4 teaspoon
ground cloves	1/4 teaspoon
unsweetened coconut cream	2 1/4 cups
chicken	3 pounds 5 ounces, cut into eight to ten pieces
unsweetened coconut milk	3 1/4 cups
tamarind puree	2 tablespoons
white vinegar	1 tablespoon
cinnamon stick	1

Wrap the shrimp paste in foil and dry-fry it with the coriander seeds, cumin seeds, and white peppercorns in a frying pan over medium-high heat for 2–3 minutes or until fragrant. Allow to cool. Using a mortar with a pestle or a spice grinder, crush or grind the coriander, cumin, and peppercorns to a powder. Process the shrimp in a small food processor until it becomes very finely shredded—forming a "floss."

Combine the crushed spices and the shrimp with the remaining curry paste ingredients in a food processor or in a mortar with a pestle. Process or pound into a smooth paste.

Heat a large saucepan or wok over medium heat. Add the coconut cream and curry paste. Stirring, cook for 20 minutes or until thick and oily. Add the chicken and the remaining ingredients and simmer gently for 50 minutes or until the chicken is tender. Season to taste and serve immediately.

Not to be confused with the juice found inside a coconut (coconut water), coconut milk/cream is the liquid obtained by pressing the grated flesh of a coconut. Traditionally, water is used in the process, with each subsequent pressing (up to three) producing a thinner milk. In countries where coconut milk is used on a daily basis, the various pressings have specific uses in cooking—a much more sophisticated use than we can get from the humble canned variety. However, it is still worth shopping around for the best—coconut milk should have a clean, white color, with the heavier cream on top, and a pleasant flavor, free of aftertaste.

thai green chicken curry .... serves 4–6

THIS DISH IS A CLASSIC OF THAI COOKING. IT IS HOT AND FRAGRANT FROM THE CURRY PASTE AND PERFUMED WITH KAFFIR LIME LEAVES AND THAI BASIL. GREEN PASTES CAN VARY, BUT THEY SHOULD BE PUNGENT RATHER THAN PIERCINGLY HOT, AND BUILT AROUND CHILIES, GALANGAL, CILANTRO, AND LEMONGRASS.

green curry paste

shrimp paste	2 teaspoons
white peppercorns	1 teaspoon
coriander seeds	2 tablespoons
cumin seeds	1 teaspoon
sea salt	1 teaspoon
lemongrass	4 stems, white part only, thinly sliced
galangal	2 teaspoons chopped
Kaffir lime leaf	1, finely shredded
cilantro	1 tablespoon chopped root
red Asian shallots	5, chopped
garlic	10 cloves, crushed
long green chilies	16, seeded, chopped
unsweetened coconut cream	17 fluid ounces, canned (do not shake the cans)
jaggery	2 tablespoons shaved (or 2 tablespoons brown sugar)
fish sauce	2 tablespoons
Kaffir lime leaves	4, finely shredded
boneless, skinless chicken thighs or breasts	2 pounds 4 ounces, cut into thick strips
bamboo shoots	3/4 cup canned, drained, sliced
yard-long beans	6, cut into 2-inch lengths
Thai basil leaves	1 handful

Wrap the shrimp paste in foil and dry-fry it with the peppercorns, coriander seeds, and cumin seeds in a frying pan over medium-high heat for 2–3 minutes or until fragrant. Allow to cool. Using a mortar with a pestle or a spice grinder, crush or grind the peppercorns, coriander, and cumin into a powder.

Put the shrimp paste and ground spices with the remaining curry paste ingredients in a food processor or in a mortar with a pestle. Process or pound into a smooth paste.

Put the thick coconut cream from the top of the cans in a saucepan. Bring to a rapid simmer over medium heat, stirring occasionally, and cook for 5–10 minutes or until the mixture "splits" (the oil starts to separate).

Add 4 tablespoons of the curry paste and simmer for 15 minutes or until fragrant. Add the jaggery, fish sauce, and lime leaves to the pan. Stir in the remaining coconut cream, the chicken, bamboo shoots, and beans. Simmer for 15 minutes or until the chicken is tender. Stir in the basil leaves and serve.

Lift off the thick coconut cream from the top of the cans.

Simmer the coconut cream until it "splits"—the oil separates.

Cook the curry paste in the coconut cream until fragrant.

fish koftas in tomato curry sauce . . . . serves 6

KOFTAS WERE ORIGINALLY INVENTED BY THE ARABS AND HAVE PROVEN TO BE IMMENSELY VERSATILE. IN THIS DISH, BOTH THE KOFTA AND THE SAUCE ARE QUITE AROMATIC; HOWEVER, THE SPICES COMPLEMENT EACH OTHER RATHER THAN COMPETE. THE SAUCE IS SLIGHTLY SWEET AND EARTHY, WHILE THE KOFTAS ARE RICH AND SPICY.

koftas

skinless, firm white fish fillets	1 pound 10 ounces, roughly chopped
onion	1, chopped
garlic	2–3 cloves, crushed
ginger	1 tablespoon grated
cilantro	4 tablespoons chopped leaves
garam masala	1 teaspoon
chili powder	1/4 teaspoon
egg	1, lightly beaten
oil	for shallow-frying

tomato curry sauce

oil	2 tablespoons
onion	1 large, finely chopped
garlic	3–4 cloves, crushed
ginger	1 tablespoon grated
ground turmeric	1 teaspoon
ground cumin	1 teaspoon
ground coriander	1 teaspoon
garam masala	1 teaspoon
chili powder	1/4 teaspoon
crushed tomatoes	28-ounce can
cilantro	3 tablespoons chopped leaves, plus extra sprigs to garnish

Put the fish in a food processor or in a mortar with a pestle, and process or pound into a smooth paste. Add the onion, garlic, ginger, cilantro leaves, garam masala, chili powder, and egg, and process or pound until well combined. Using wetted hands, form 1 tablespoon of the fish mixture into a ball. Repeat with the remaining mixture.

To make the tomato curry sauce, heat the oil in a large saucepan. Add the onion, garlic, and ginger. Stirring frequently, cook over medium heat for 8 minutes or until lightly golden. Add the spices and cook, stirring, for 2 minutes or until aromatic. Add the tomatoes and 1 cup water, then reduce the heat and simmer, stirring frequently, for 15 minutes or until the sauce reduces and thickens.

Meanwhile, heat the oil in a large frying pan to a depth of 3/4 inch. Add the fish koftas in three or four batches and cook for 3 minutes or until browned all over. Drain on paper towels.

Add the koftas to the sauce and simmer over low heat for 5 minutes or until heated through. Gently fold in the chopped cilantro, season with salt, and serve garnished with cilantro sprigs.

thai basil, beef, and green peppercorn curry .... serves 4

TWO INGREDIENTS IN THIS DISH MAKE IT DISTINCTLY THAI (THREE IF WE INCLUDE THE CURRY PASTE). THE FIRST IS THAI BASIL, WITH ITS DISTINCTIVE PERFUME AND CLEAN FLAVOR. THE SECOND IS PICKLED GREEN PEPPERCORNS. THEY ADD A SALTY, VINEGARY, SLIGHTLY SWEET QUALITY, WITHOUT TOO MUCH HEAT.

ginger	2 tablespoons grated
garlic	2 cloves, crushed
rump or round steak	1 pound 2 ounces
unsweetened coconut cream	1 cup
yellow curry paste	1 tablespoon, store-bought or see recipe on page 41
fish sauce	1/3 cup
jaggery	1/3 cup shaved (or 1/3 cup brown sugar)
lemongrass	2 stems, white part only, finely chopped
galangal	1 thick slice
Kaffir lime leaves	4
tomatoes	2, cut into 3/4-inch cubes
large bamboo pieces	14-ounce can, drained, cut into small chunks
Thai pickled green peppercorns	8 stems
tamarind puree	2 tablespoons
Thai basil leaves	1 large handful, chopped

Crush the ginger and garlic to a rough pulp in a mortar with a pestle or food processor. Cut the meat into strips 2 x 3/4-inch and 1/8-inch thick. Toss the ginger and garlic paste together with the beef and marinate for 30 minutes.

Bring half the coconut cream to a boil in a flameproof casserole dish over medium heat, then reduce to a simmer. Stir in the yellow curry paste and cook for 3–5 minutes. Add the fish sauce and jaggery, and stir until the jaggery dissolves.

Increase the heat to high. Add all the remaining ingredients (except the remaining coconut cream) and 1 1/2 cups water. Bring to a boil, then reduce the heat and simmer uncovered for 1–1 1/4 hours or until the beef is tender.

Check the seasoning and correct by adding extra fish sauce or jaggery if necessary. Stir in the remaining coconut cream and serve immediately.

Pound the ginger and garlic together into a rough pulp.

Stir in the yellow curry paste and cook until aromatic.

Add the jaggery to the mixture and stir until dissolved.

five-spice pork curry . . . . serves 4

THIS DISH DRAWS ON VARIOUS INFLUENCES TO CREATE A SPICY, SALTY, AND FRAGRANT DISH. FIVE-SPICE IS WIDELY USED IN MANY ASIAN COUNTRIES BESIDES CHINA, AND HERE IT IS MIXED WITH KECAP MANIS, A THICK, SWEET, DARK SOY SAUCE FROM INDONESIA. FIVE-SPICE IS STRONGLY FLAVORED, SO USE SPARINGLY.

pork spareribs	1 pound 2 ounces
oil	1 1/2 tablespoons
garlic	2 cloves, crushed
fried tofu puffs	6 (about 7 ounces)
ginger	1 tablespoon finely chopped
five-spice	1 teaspoon
ground white pepper	1/2 teaspoon
fish sauce	3 tablespoons
kecap manis	3 tablespoons
light soy sauce	2 tablespoons
jaggery	1/4 cup shaved
	(or 1/4 cup brown sugar)
cilantro	1 small handful leaves, chopped
snow peas	1 1/4 cups, thinly sliced

Cut the pork spareribs into 1-inch thick pieces, discarding any small pieces of bone. Put the pork ribs into a saucepan and cover with cold water. Bring to a boil, then reduce to a simmer and cook for 5 minutes. Drain and set aside.

Heat the oil in a heavy-based saucepan over medium-high heat. Add the pork and garlic, and stir until lightly browned. Add the remaining ingredients, except the snow peas, then pour in 2 1/4 cups water. Cover and bring to a boil. Then reduce to a simmer and cook, stirring occasionally, for 15–18 minutes or until the pork is tender. Stir in the snow peas and serve.

Five-spice originated in China, though it is now used in many parts of Southeast Asia. It contains ground star anise, fennel seeds, cassia or cinnamon, Szechuan pepper, and cloves. As with all spice blends, proportions vary depending on the cook, though generally the star anise dominates. In some versions, five-spice is not five at all but six- or seven-spice— ginger and/or cardamom may sneak in. This blend is pungent and quite potent, so a little goes a long way. It is used in marinades for meat, fish, or poultry—its most famous use is in the marinade for Peking duck—and also with vegetables, in stir-fries, and even on fruit.

three ways with tomatoes

A JUICY BURST OF RIPE TOMATO ON THE PALATE CAN BE JUST THE THING WHEN EATING A CURRY. SWEET, CLEANSING, AND REFRESHING, IT IS AN IDEAL INGREDIENT FOR A RELISH. IN THE FIRST RELISH HERE IT IS COMBINED WITH LIVELY MINT AND LIME; IN THE SECOND, WITH FRESH CILANTRO AND GREEN CHILIES. INDIAN PICKLES ARE DIFFERENT CREATURES: DESIGNED TO STIMULATE THE PALATE, THEY ARE COOKED IN OIL WITH LITTLE OR NO SUGAR, AND ARE SHARP, SPICY, AND STRONGLY FLAVORED.

tomato, lime, and mint relish

Peel 1 lime, removing all white pith. Finely dice and put into a nonreactive bowl with 2 diced tomatoes, 1 thinly sliced scallion, 2 tablespoons chopped mint, 1 teaspoon fish sauce, 1 teaspoon coconut vinegar (fermented coconut sap), and 1 teaspoon shaved jaggery. Stir to combine and let sit covered in the refrigerator 30 minutes before serving. This relish goes well with spicy Thai curries. Serves 4.

tomato and cilantro relish

Mix together 2 diced tomatoes, 3 thinly sliced scallions, 2 tablespoons finely chopped cilantro leaves, 1 thinly sliced green chili, 1 tablespoon lemon juice, and 1 teaspoon soft brown sugar. Season with salt and pepper and let sit covered in the refrigerator 30 minutes before serving. This relish goes well with Indian and Thai curries. Serves 4.

indian tomato oil pickle

Put 2 teaspoons black or brown mustard seeds and $1/3$ cup cider vinegar in a small saucepan, and heat over low heat for 12 minutes or until the seeds just start to pop. The vinegar will be nearly evaporated. Allow to cool. Put the seeds, 1 tablespoon grated ginger, and 5 chopped garlic cloves in a food processor or in a mortar with a pestle. Process or pound into a smooth paste. Heat 3 tablespoons oil in a saucepan. Add 3 teaspoons ground cumin and 2 teaspoons ground turmeric. Stirring gently, cook over low heat for 4 minutes or until fragrant. Add the mustard seed mixture; 1 teaspoon chili powder; 8 peeled, seeded, and chopped firm, ripe tomatoes; 3 tablespoons sugar; and 1 teaspoon salt. Reduce the heat and simmer, stirring occasionally, for 45 minutes or until thick. Stir in 1 extra tablespoon cider vinegar. Spoon into clean, warm jars, seal, and cool. Refrigerate for up to one month. This pickle is best served with Indian curries. Serves 6.

paneer and pea curry .... serves 5

THIS SUBSTANTIAL YET FRAGRANT DISH IS AN EXCELLENT STARTING POINT FOR A VEGETARIAN MEAL. PANEER IS AN INDIAN COTTAGE CHEESE THAT IS MADE BY HEATING AND CURDLING MILK, THEN SEPARATING THE SOLIDS. IT SHOULD ALWAYS BE MADE FRESH, AS IT LASTS ONLY A FEW DAYS, THOUGH IT CAN BE BOUGHT READY-MADE.

paneer

milk	8 cups
lemon juice	1/3 cup
oil	for deep-frying

curry paste

onions	2 large
garlic	3 cloves
ginger	1 teaspoon grated
cumin seeds	1 teaspoon
dried red chilies	3
cardamom seeds	1 teaspoon
cloves	4
fennel seeds	1 teaspoon
cassia bark	2 pieces

peas	3 1/4 cups
oil	2 tablespoons
pureed tomatoes	1 2/3 cups
garam masala	1 tablespoon
ground coriander	1 teaspoon
ground turmeric	1/4 teaspoon
whipping cream	1 tablespoon
cilantro	leaves, to serve

Put the milk in a large saucepan, bring to a boil, then stir in the lemon juice and turn off the heat. Stir the mixture for 1–2 seconds as it curdles. Put in a strainer and leave for 30 minutes for the whey to drain off. Place the paneer curds on a clean, flat surface, cover with a plate to weigh down, and leave for at least 4 hours.

Combine all the curry paste ingredients in a food processor or in a mortar with a pestle, and process or pound to a smooth paste.

Cut the solid paneer into 3/4-inch cubes. Fill a deep, heavy-based saucepan one-third full of oil and heat to 350°F or until a cube of bread browns in 15 seconds. Cook the paneer in batches for 2–3 minutes or until golden. Drain on paper towels.

Bring a saucepan of water to a boil, add the peas, and cook for 3 minutes or until tender. Drain and set aside.

Heat the oil in a large saucepan, add the curry paste, and cook over medium heat for 4 minutes, or until fragrant. Add the tomatoes, spices, cream, and 1/2 cup water. Season with salt and simmer over medium heat for 5 minutes. Add the paneer and peas, and cook for 3 minutes. Garnish with cilantro leaves and serve.

Strain for 30 minutes to help dry out the curds.

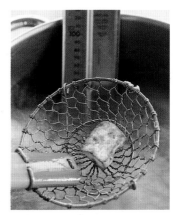

Deep-fry the paneer cubes in batches until golden.

kenyan cilantro lamb

serves 6

MUCH OF KENYAN CUISINE IS FAIRLY SIMPLE, SO IT IS A SURPRISE TO COME ACROSS INDIAN SPICES AND ARABIAN AND PORTUGUESE INFLUENCES IN A CURRY. BUT THE SWAHILI CUISINE OF THE KENYAN COAST IS JUST SUCH A VIBRANT FUSION, USING INTRODUCED AND LOCAL INGREDIENTS TO PRODUCE COLORFUL AND RICHLY SPICED DISHES.

garlic	4 cloves, crushed
ginger	1 1/2 tablespoons chopped
lemon juice	2 1/2 tablespoons
lamb leg or shoulder	2 pounds 4 ounces, diced
coriander seeds	1 1/2 tablespoons
black peppercorns	1/4 teaspoon
tomatoes	2, chopped
tomato paste	2 teaspoons
long green chilies	3, seeded, chopped
cilantro	1 handful stalks and roots, roughly chopped
oil	3 tablespoons
chicken stock	1 cup
plain yogurt	2 tablespoons
cilantro	1 large handful leaves, finely chopped, to serve

Combine the garlic, ginger, lemon juice, and enough water to form a paste in a food processor or in a mortar with a pestle. Process or pound into a smooth paste. Put the lamb into a nonreactive bowl, add the garlic paste, and combine well. Cover and refrigerate for 2 hours.

Dry-fry the coriander seeds and peppercorns in a frying pan over medium-high heat for 2–3 minutes or until fragrant. Allow to cool. Using a mortar with a pestle or a spice grinder, crush or grind into a powder.

Put the ground spices, tomatoes, tomato paste, chilies, and cilantro stalks and roots in a food processor or in a mortar with a pestle, and process or pound to a smooth paste.

Heat the oil in a heavy-based saucepan over medium-high heat and brown the lamb in batches. When all the lamb is cooked, return to the pan with the tomato chili paste and the stock. Bring to a boil. Then reduce to a slow simmer, cover, and cook for 1 1/2 hours. Remove the lid and cook for an additional 15 minutes or until the lamb is very tender. While cooking, skim and discard any oil that surfaces.

Remove from the heat and gently stir in the yogurt, garnish with cilantro leaves, and serve.

Process the garlic, ginger, and lemon juice until smooth.

Process the spices with the tomatoes and tomato paste.

Brown the lamb in batches before adding the tomato chili paste.

spicy chicken and tomato curry............................serves 8–10

THIS RECIPE LEAVES BARELY A SPICE UNTOUCHED! CONTAINING SPICES THAT RANGE FROM HOT TO SWEET, SHARP TO GENTLY PERFUMED, THIS IS A DISH IN WHICH THE CHICKEN SUPPORTS THE FLAVORINGS, NOT THE OTHER WAY AROUND. IT IS ALSO A SIMPLE DISH TO PREPARE.

oil	1 tablespoon
chickens	two 3-pound 5-ounce, jointed
onion	1, sliced
ground cloves	1/2 teaspoon
ground turmeric	1 teaspoon
garam masala	2 teaspoons
chili powder	3 teaspoons
cardamom pods	3
garlic	3 cloves, crushed
ginger	1 tablespoon grated
poppy seeds	1 tablespoon
fennel seeds	2 teaspoons
unsweetened coconut milk	1 cup
star anise	1
cinnamon stick	1
tomatoes	4 large, roughly chopped
lime juice	2 tablespoons

Heat the oil in a large frying pan over medium heat. Add the chicken in batches and cook for 5–10 minutes or until browned. Transfer to a large saucepan.

Add the onion to the frying pan and cook, stirring, for about 10 minutes or until golden. Stir in the ground cloves, turmeric, garam masala, and chili powder. Stirring, cook for 1 minute. Add to the chicken in the saucepan.

Lightly crush the cardamom pods with the flat side of a heavy knife. Remove the seeds and discard the pods. Combine the seeds and the garlic, ginger, poppy seeds, fennel seeds, and 2 tablespoons of the coconut milk in a food processor or in a mortar with a pestle. Process or pound into a smooth paste. Add the spice paste, the remaining coconut milk, star anise, cinnamon stick, tomatoes, and 3 tablespoons water to the chicken.

Simmer covered for 45 minutes or until the chicken is tender. Remove the chicken, cover, and keep warm. Boil the cooking liquid for 20–25 minutes or until reduced by half. Put the chicken on a serving plate, mix the lime juice with the cooking liquid, and pour over the chicken.

Brown the chicken in the frying pan in batches.

Fry the onions until golden before adding the spices.

thai green curry with fish balls . . . . serves 4

A LONG-TIME THAI FAVORITE, THIS DISH FEATURES FISH BALLS OR DUMPLINGS RATHER THAN PIECES OF FISH (HOWEVER, SLICES OF FISH CAN ALSO BE USED). THAI EGGPLANTS, GALANGAL, AND TANGY KAFFIR LIME LEAVES ADD DEPTH TO THE SPICY CURRY BASE, WHILE THE POUNDED FISH PROVIDES TEXTURE.

skinless, firm white fish fillets	12 ounces, roughly cut into pieces
unsweetened coconut cream	3 tablespoons
green curry paste	2 tablespoons, store-bought or see recipe on page 130
unsweetened coconut milk	1³/4 cups, plus extra for topping
Thai apple eggplants	4, quartered
pea eggplants	20–30
fish sauce	2 tablespoons
jaggery	2 tablespoons shaved (or 2 tablespoons brown sugar)
galangal	1¹/2-inch piece, thinly sliced
Kaffir lime leaves	3, torn in half
holy basil leaves	1 handful, to serve
long red chili	1/2, seeded, thinly sliced, to serve

Put the fish fillets in a food processor or in a mortar with a pestle, and process or pound into a smooth paste.

Put the coconut cream in a saucepan, bring to a rapid simmer over medium heat. Stirring occasionally, cook for 5–10 minutes or until the mixture "splits" (the oil starts to separate). Add the curry paste and cook for 5 minutes or until fragrant. Add the coconut milk and mix well.

Use a spoon or your wet hands to shape the fish paste into small balls, about ³/4-inch across, then drop them into the coconut milk. Add the Thai apple eggplants, pea eggplants, fish sauce, and jaggery. Cook for 15 minutes, stirring occasionally until the eggplant and fish balls are cooked.

Stir in the galangal and the lime leaves. Taste, then adjust the seasoning if necessary. Spoon into a serving bowl and sprinkle with extra coconut milk, basil leaves, and sliced chili.

Process the skinless fish fillets into a smooth paste.

Stir the paste into the coconut cream and cook until fragrant.

Shape the fish paste into small balls with wet hands.

shrimp with thai basil

THIS FRAGRANT AND TASTY CURRY COULDN'T BE EASIER TO MAKE. ONCE THE SHRIMP ARE PREPARED, THE COOKING TAKES ONLY MINUTES. THE SAUCE SHOULD BE THICK, HOT, AND SWEET, SO MAKE SURE YOUR SAUCEPAN OR WOK IS HOT ENOUGH TO REDUCE THE COCONUT MILK AS SOON AS IT IS ADDED.

curry paste

dried long red chilies	2
lemongrass	2 stems, white part only, thinly sliced
galangal	1-inch piece, thinly sliced
garlic	5 cloves, crushed
red Asian shallots	4, finely chopped
cilantro	6 roots, finely chopped
shrimp paste	1 teaspoon
ground cumin	1 teaspoon
unsalted peanuts	3 tablespoons, chopped
raw shrimp	1 pound 5 ounces, peeled, deveined, tails intact
oil	2 tablespoons
unsweetened coconut milk	3/4 cup
fish sauce	2 teaspoons
jaggery	2 teaspoons shaved (or 2 teaspoons brown sugar)
Thai basil leaves	1 handful, to serve

Soak the chilies in boiling water for 5 minutes or until soft. Remove the seeds and stems, then chop. Combine the chilies and the remaining curry paste ingredients in a food processor or in a mortar with a pestle. Process or pound into a smooth paste.

Cut each shrimp along the back so it opens like a butterfly (leave each one joined along the base and at the tail).

Heat the oil in a saucepan or wok and stir-fry 2 tablespoons of the curry paste over medium heat for 2 minutes or until fragrant. Add the coconut milk, fish sauce, and jaggery and cook for a few seconds. Add the shrimp and cook for a few minutes or until cooked through. Taste, then adjust the seasoning if necessary. Serve garnished with basil leaves.

Three main types of basil are used in Thai cuisine. The most important by far is Thai basil, also known as Thai sweet basil. This variety has purplish stems, lush, deep-green leaves, and an aniseed aroma and flavor. It is added liberally to a wide range of dishes. Next up is holy basil, which is available in two types: red- and white-stemmed. Highly perfumed and with a peppery taste, holy basil is always cooked to release its flavor. The final type is lemon basil, also called mint basil. As its name suggests, it has a fresh, tangy scent and flavor and is delicious with fish, poultry, and sweet drinks and desserts.

lamb and spinach curry .... serves 6

THIS IS A RICHLY FLAVORED, TRADITIONAL DISH FROM THE PUNJABI REGION OF NORTHERN INDIA. IT IS COOKED UNTIL THE SAUCE IS VERY THICK AND FAIRLY DRY. THE DISTINCTIVE FLAVORS OF THE LAMB AND SPINACH BLEND TO FORM A SMOOTH, UNIFIED WHOLE. IT CAN BE SERVED WITH EITHER RICE OR BREADS.

coriander seeds	2 teaspoons
cumin seeds	1 1/2 teaspoons
oil	3 tablespoons
leg or shoulder of lamb	2 pounds 4 ounces boneless, cut into 1-inch cubes
onions	4, finely chopped
cloves	6
cardamom pods	6
cinnamon stick	1
black peppercorns	10
Indian bay (cassia) leaves	4
garam masala	3 teaspoons
ground turmeric	1/4 teaspoon
paprika	1 teaspoon
ginger	2 1/2-inch piece, grated
garlic cloves	4, crushed
Greek-style yogurt	3/4 cup (or plain yogurt drained in cheesecloth)
spinach (or amaranth) leaves	4 1/2 cups, roughly chopped

Dry-fry the coriander and cumin seeds in a frying pan over medium-high heat for 2–3 minutes or until fragrant. Allow to cool. Using a mortar with a pestle or a spice grinder, crush or grind into a powder.

Heat the oil in a flameproof casserole dish over low heat and fry a few pieces of meat at a time until browned. Remove from the dish. Add more oil to the dish if necessary, and fry the onion, cloves, cardamom pods, cinnamon stick, black peppercorns, and bay leaves until the onion is lightly browned. Add the ground cumin and coriander, the garam masala, turmeric, and paprika and fry for 30 seconds.

Return the meat to the dish and add the ginger, garlic, yogurt, and 1 2/3 cups water. Bring to a boil. Reduce the heat to a simmer, cover, and cook for 1 1/2–2 hours or until the meat is very tender. At this stage, most of the water should have evaporated. If not, remove the lid, increase the heat, and cook until the moisture evaporates.

Cook the spinach leaves briefly in a little simmering water until just wilted, then refresh in cold water. Drain thoroughly, then finely chop. Squeeze out any extra water. Add the spinach to the lamb and cook for 3 minutes or until the spinach and the lamb are well mixed and any extra liquid has evaporated.

green herb pork curry .... serves 6

A GENEROUS USE OF CILANTRO AND DILL MIXED WITH YOGURT AND ADDED AT THE LAST MINUTE TO THE CURRY GIVES THIS DISH A BURST OF FRESH HERB FLAVOR. BALANCING THIS ARE THE WARMER, ROUNDER, ROASTED AROMAS OF FENNEL AND CORIANDER SEEDS.

coriander seeds	2 teaspoons
fennel seeds	2 teaspoons
ground white pepper	1/4 teaspoon
ginger	1 1/2 tablespoons grated
garlic	6 cloves, crushed
onions	2, chopped
oil	3 tablespoons
pork shoulder	2 pounds 4 ounces, cut into 3/4-inch cubes
chicken stock	1 cup
plain yogurt	1/2 cup
cilantro	1 large handful leaves, roughly chopped
dill	1 large handful, roughly chopped

Dry-fry the coriander and fennel seeds in a frying pan over medium-high heat for 2–3 minutes or until fragrant. Allow to cool. Using a mortar with a pestle or a spice grinder, crush or grind into a powder.

Combine the ground coriander and fennel seeds with the pepper, ginger, garlic, and onion in a food processor or in a mortar with a pestle. Process or pound into a smooth paste. Add a little water if it is too thick.

Heat 2 tablespoons of the oil in a heavy-based saucepan over high heat, and brown the pork in batches. Set aside. Reduce the heat to low, then add the remaining oil and cook the spice and onion paste, stirring constantly, for 5–8 minutes. Add the pork back to the pan, and stir to coat with the paste. Add the stock, increase the heat to high, and bring to a boil. Then reduce to a very slow simmer, cover, and cook for 2–2 1/2 hours or until the pork is very tender. While cooking, stir occasionally and skim and discard any oil that surfaces.

Put the yogurt, cilantro, dill, and 3 tablespoons of the cooking liquid from the pork into a pitcher or bowl and blend with a hand blender until smooth. Stir the yogurt mixture into the pork. Remove from the heat, season well to taste, and serve.

Process the onion mixture to a smooth paste.

Stir the pork into the paste mixture, coating well.

Blend the yogurt, herbs, and cooking liquid until smooth.

chicken masala .... serves 4

MASALA SIMPLY MEANS "MIXTURE OF SPICES," A CATCHALL WORD THAT COULD BE USED WITH JUST ABOUT ANY CURRY. IN THIS CASE, THE MIXTURE IS AROMATIC BUT ONLY MODERATELY SPICY, GIVING THE DISH A SUBTLE FLAVOR. THE COMBINATION OF TOMATOES AND GINGER ADDS A DELICIOUS EXTRA FLAVORING TO THE SPICES.

boneless, skinless chicken thighs	3 pounds 5 ounces
ground cumin	2 teaspoons
ground coriander	2 teaspoons
garam masala	1 1/2 teaspoons
ground turmeric	1/4 teaspoon
onions	2, finely chopped
garlic	4 cloves, roughly chopped
ginger	2-inch piece, roughly chopped
tomatoes	2 ripe, chopped
ghee or oil	3 tablespoons
cloves	5
cardamom pods	8, bruised
cinnamon stick	1
curry leaves	10
Greek-style yogurt	2/3 cup (or plain yogurt drained in cheesecloth)

Trim off any excess fat from the chicken. Mix the cumin, coriander, garam masala, and turmeric together and rub it into the chicken.

Combine half the onion with the garlic, ginger, and tomatoes in a food processor or in a mortar with a pestle. Process or pound into a smooth paste.

Heat the ghee or oil in a flameproof casserole dish over low heat, add the remaining onion, cloves, cardamom, cinnamon stick, and curry leaves. Fry until the onion is golden brown. Add the tomatoes and onion paste and stir for 5 minutes. Season with salt to taste. Add the yogurt and whisk until smooth, then add the spiced chicken. Toss the chicken pieces in the mixture, then bring slowly to a boil.

Reduce the heat, cover, and simmer for 50 minutes or until the oil separates from the sauce. Stir the ingredients occasionally to prevent the chicken from sticking. If the sauce is too thin, simmer for a couple of minutes with the lid off.

Cinnamon is familiar to us all as quills of delicate, tightly rolled, light brown layers of paper-thin bark. It is indigenous to Sri Lanka, and the world's best still comes from there. As with many spices, early traders invented fanciful tales to hide its origins and many struggles have been waged over its control. In its homeland, only a caste known as the Chalais could harvest and peel the spice. Today, we can easily buy the quills, but its sweet, inviting fragrance and taste still conjure up an exotic past. Cinnamon is used in dishes ranging from milk puddings to pickles, and is essential in spice blends such as garam masala.

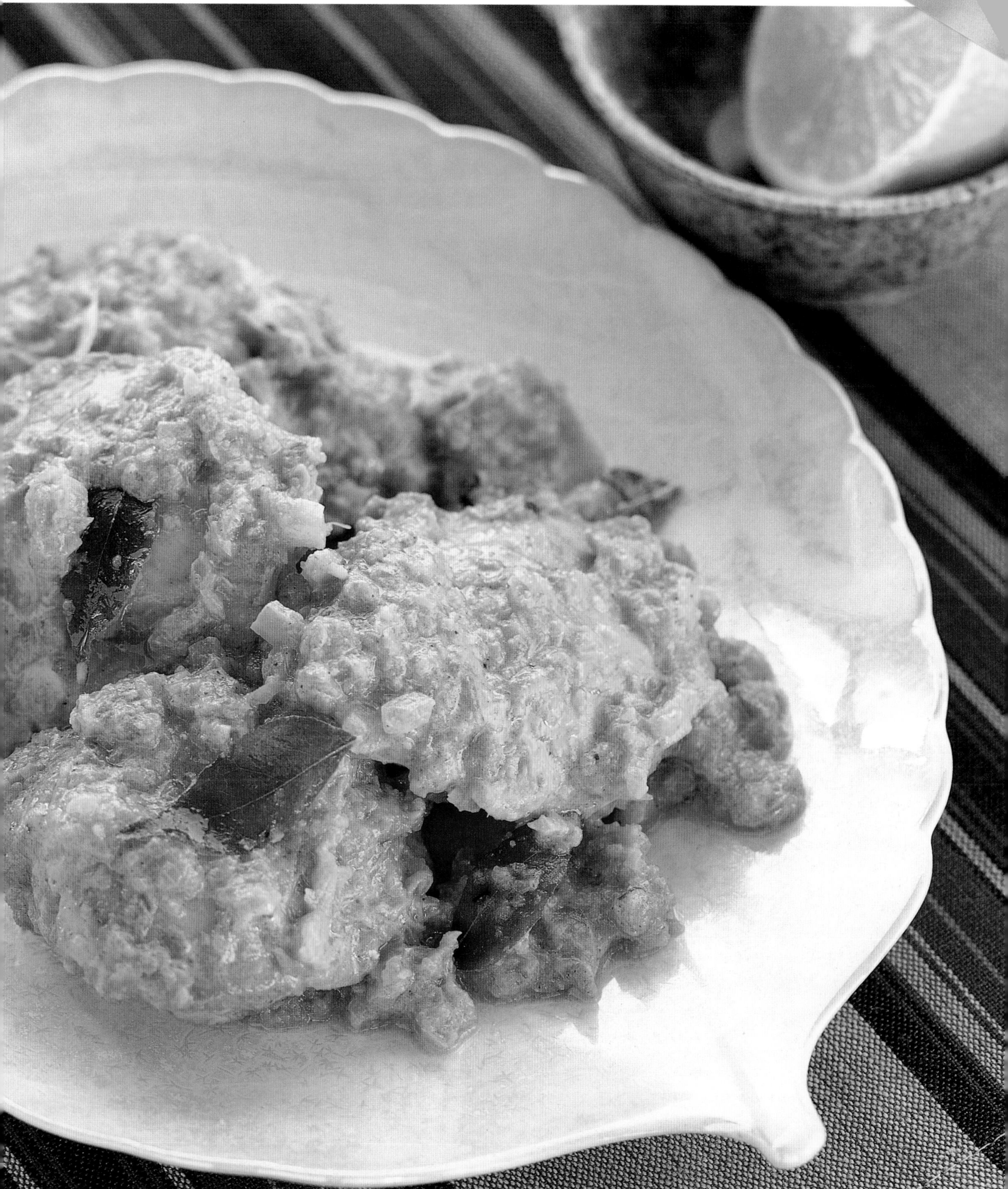

softly sweet

It is interesting how certain ingredients, though now familiar to us all, retain the sense of luxury that they held in earlier times. This seems especially true of sweet spices such as cinnamon, saffron, and cardamom, but also of ingredients such as almonds and raisins—just a sprinkle adds a touch of festivity to a dish. This chapter looks at the wide range of ingredients that are used in curries to give them a gentle sweetness, such as pineapple, apricots, orange juice, honey, and mint.

Many of the sweet flavors in the following dishes come from introduced ingredients, and it is a testament to the versatility of curries that they can absorb new ingredients and very successfully make them their own. For example, the chili, native to Central America, could not be more at home in the curries of India and Southeast Asia. But this is true also of perfumed lychees from China, sweet almonds from Persia, and juicy tomatoes from South America. Barbecued duck curry with lychees has two of China's most famous ingredients, here seamlessly blended with classic curry spices such as cumin, paprika, turmeric, and ground coriander, as well as the ever-present coconut cream, fish sauce, and jaggery. Minted lamb curry transfers the classic combination of fresh, sweet mint and lamb to the world of spicy curries, complementing the fresh herb taste with green chilies, tart lemon juice, and sharp cayenne pepper and turmeric.

Sweet ingredients also provide the perfect opportunity for including robust flavors, such as duck and pork, but also seasonings like Indonesia's hot and spicy sambal oelek, and fruits such as green bananas. As when blending hot and sour ingredients, sweet and robust flavors are used to complement each other, not compete. An Indian pork, honey, and almond curry included here also contains fresh herbs, citrus zest, spices, and yogurt, all brought magically together through slow, gentle cooking. Snapper with green bananas and mango is another excellent, delicious example of the art of balance that is so central to all curries. The starchy bananas provide texture and act as a thickening agent, the mango contributes a lovely summery sweetness, and the fish just absorbs it all, supported by a spicy yellow curry paste and rich coconut cream base. This chapter may appear less traditional than others in this book but it still follows the principles of cooking curries that make these dishes so popular the world over.

barbecued duck curry with lychees . . . . serves 4

THIS COLORFUL CURRY FEATURES THE DELICATE APPEAL OF LYCHEES. NATIVE TO CHINA BUT NOW GROWN IN SOUTHEAST ASIA AND INDIA, LYCHEES HAVE A CREAMY, SWEET FLESH AND GENTLE PERFUME. THE SPICE PASTE IS EARTHY AND PEPPERY, RATHER THAN HOT, AND BALANCES WELL WITH THE RICH-TASTING MEAT AND COCONUT.

curry paste

shrimp paste	1 teaspoon
white peppercorns	1 teaspoon
long red chilies	3, seeded
red onion	1, roughly chopped
garlic	2 cloves
lemongrass	2 stems, white part only, thinly sliced
ginger	2-inch piece
cilantro	3 roots
Kaffir lime leaves	5
oil	2 tablespoons
ground coriander	2 teaspoons
ground cumin	1 teaspoon
paprika	1 teaspoon
ground turmeric	1 teaspoon
Chinese barbecued duck	1 (see notes)
unsweetened coconut cream	14 fluid-ounce can (do not shake the can)
jaggery	1 tablespoon shaved (or 1 tablespoon brown sugar)
fish sauce	2 tablespoons
galangal	1 thick slice
straw mushrooms	8½-ounce can, drained
lychees	14-ounce can, cut in half, (reserve ¼ cup syrup)
cherry tomatoes	2 cups
Thai basil leaves	1 handful, chopped
cilantro	1 handful leaves, chopped

Wrap the shrimp paste in foil and dry-fry it with the peppercorns in a frying pan over medium-high heat for 2–3 minutes or until fragrant. Allow to cool. Using a mortar with a pestle or a spice grinder, crush or grind the peppercorns into a powder. Put the crushed peppercorns and the shrimp with the remaining curry paste ingredients in a food processor or in a mortar with a pestle. Process or pound into a smooth paste.

Remove the duck meat from the bones and chop into bite-size pieces. Put the thick coconut cream from the top of the can in a saucepan, bring to a rapid simmer over medium heat, and, stirring occasionally, cook for 5–10 minutes or until the mixture "splits" (the oil starts to separate). Add half the curry paste, jaggery, and fish sauce, and stir until the jaggery dissolves. Add the duck, galangal, straw mushrooms, lychees, reserved lychee syrup, and remaining coconut cream. Bring to a boil, then reduce to a simmer and cook for 15–20 minutes.

Add the tomatoes, basil, and cilantro. Season to taste. Serve when the cherry tomatoes soften slightly.

Notes: Chinese barbecued ducks can be purchased from Chinese restaurants. When in season, you can use fresh lychees, which will be sweeter and juicier than the canned variety, so you won't need to use the added syrup.

Process all the curry paste ingredients until smooth.

Remove the duck meat from the bones and chop.

chicken, almond, and raisin curry

....serves 6

WHILE THE CHICKEN COOKS, YOU WILL BE ABLE TO SAVOR THE WONDERFUL AROMAS COMING FROM THIS SWEETLY SPICED CURRY. THE DISH FEATURES RELATIVELY FEW SPICES, BUT THEY ARE IN PERFECT HARMONY WITH EACH OTHER: CLOVES AND GINGER PROVIDE SHARPNESS, WHILE THE ALMONDS AND RAISINS ADD A TOUCH OF LUXURY.

cardamom pods	6
cloves	6
cumin seeds	1 teaspoon
cayenne pepper	1/2 teaspoon
ghee or oil	2 tablespoons
boneless, skinless chicken thighs	2 pounds 4 ounces, cut into 11/4-inch cubes
onion	1, finely chopped
garlic	3 cloves, crushed
ginger	11/2 tablespoons finely grated
cinnamon sticks	2
bay leaves	2
blanched almonds	1/3 cup, lightly toasted
raisins	1/3 cup
plain yogurt	1 cup
chicken stock	1/2 cup

Lightly crush the cardamom pods with the flat side of a heavy knife. Remove the seeds and discard the pods. Dry-fry the seeds along with the cloves, cumin seeds, and cayenne pepper in a frying pan over medium-high heat for 2–3 minutes or until fragrant. Allow to cool. Using a mortar with a pestle or a spice grinder, crush or grind into a powder.

In a large, heavy-based frying pan, heat the ghee or oil over medium-high heat. Brown the chicken in batches and set aside. In the same pan, cook the onion, garlic, and ginger over low heat for 5–8 minutes until softened. Add the ground spice mix, cinnamon sticks, and bay leaves. Stirring constantly, cook for 5 minutes. Put the almonds, raisins, and chicken into the pan. Add the yogurt a spoonful at a time, stirring to incorporate it into the dish. Add the stock, reduce the heat to low, then cover and cook for 40 minutes or until the chicken is tender. While cooking, skim and discard any oil that surfaces. Season well and serve.

First introduced to India by the Persian Moguls, almonds remain a highly valued ingredient. Fragrant and creamy, they are used in coconut- or yogurt-based curries and in Indian drinks and desserts, including the famous kulfi. The almond tree is suited to Mediterranean-style climates, so is grown only as far east as Kashmir, contributing to its allure. Almonds are available whole with skins on or blanched, chopped, slivered, flaked, or ground. Use only blanched nuts in curries: to blanch, pour boiling water over them and let sit for 2 minutes. Drain and slip off the skins. To toast, spread the nuts on a baking sheet and cook at 350°F for 8–10 minutes.

indian pork, honey, and almond curry
serves 4

THIS UNUSUAL CURRY BLENDS AROMATIC CINNAMON AND CARDAMOM WITH SWEET HONEY AND ALMONDS, FRAGRANT CITRUS, AND THE FRESH LIVELINESS OF PARSLEY AND CILANTRO. PORK IS THE PERFECT CHOICE FOR THIS MIX OF AROMAS AND FLAVORS, COMPLEMENTING RATHER THAN BEING SWAMPED BY THEM.

cinnamon stick	1
cardamom pods	3
boneless pork shoulder	1 pound 10 ounces
oil	1 tablespoon
honey	2 tablespoons
garlic	3 cloves, crushed
onions	2, chopped
chicken stock	2/3 cup
ground turmeric	1 teaspoon
ground black pepper	1/2 teaspoon
lemon zest	1 teaspoon grated
orange zest	1 teaspoon grated
plain yogurt	1 cup
slivered almonds	1/4 cup, toasted
cilantro	1 small handful leaves, chopped
Italian parsley	1 small handful, chopped

Dry-fry the cinnamon stick and cardamom in a frying pan over medium-high heat for 2–3 minutes or until fragrant. Allow to cool. Using a mortar with a pestle or a spice grinder, crush or grind into a powder.

Cut the pork into 3/4-inch cubes. Heat the oil and honey in a heavy-based saucepan over medium heat. Add the cubed pork, garlic, and onion, and cook for 8–10 minutes or until the onion is translucent and the pork is light golden. Add 3/4 cup water and the chicken stock, bring to a boil, then reduce to a simmer. Cover and cook, stirring occasionally, for 1 1/4 hours or until the pork is tender.

Uncover and bring to a rapid simmer for 10 minutes or until most of the liquid is absorbed. Add the ground spices, turmeric, pepper, citrus zest, and 1 teaspoon salt, and simmer for an additional 3–4 minutes. To serve, gently reheat, stirring in the yogurt, almonds, cilantro, and parsley.

Cut the boneless pork shoulder into neat cubes.

Sauté the pork for 8–10 minutes or until it becomes lightly golden.

Stir in the spices, grated citrus zest, and salt. Simmer.

butternut squash and spinach curry... serves 6

THIS CURRY CONTAINS SOME OF THE CLASSIC INGREDIENTS OF INDONESIAN COOKING, INCLUDING CANDLENUTS, SHALLOTS, GALANGAL, AND SAMBAL OELEK. *SAMBAL* MEANS HOT AND SPICY—WHICH GIVES YOU AN IDEA OF THE DISH'S TASTE. THIS PARTICULAR SAMBAL IS AN UNCOOKED MIXTURE OF CHILIES, SALT, AND VINEGAR OR CITRUS.

curry paste

candlenuts	3
raw peanuts	1 tablespoon
red Asian shallots	3, chopped
garlic	2 cloves
sambal oelek	2–3 teaspoons
ground turmeric	1/4 teaspoon
galangal	1 teaspoon grated
oil	2 tablespoons
onion	1, finely chopped
butternut squash	4 cups, cut into 3/4-inch cubes
vegetable stock	1/2 cup (or as required)
spinach	4 cups, roughly chopped
unsweetened coconut cream	14 fluid-ounce can, or 1 2/3 cups
sugar	1/4 teaspoon

Combine all the curry paste ingredients in a food processor or in a mortar with a pestle, and process or pound into a smooth paste.

Heat the oil in a large saucepan, add the curry paste, and cook, stirring, over low heat for 3–5 minutes or until fragrant. Add the onion and cook for another 5 minutes or until softened.

Add the squash and half the vegetable stock. Cook covered for 10 minutes or until the squash is almost cooked through. Add more stock, if required. Add the spinach, coconut cream, and sugar to the pan. Season with salt. Bring to a boil, stirring constantly, then reduce the heat and simmer for 3–5 minutes or until the spinach is cooked and the sauce thickens slightly. Serve immediately.

Process all the paste ingredients to form a smooth paste.

Stir the onion into the paste and cook until softened.

Add the squash with the stock and cook until almost tender.

ground lamb with orange . . . . serves 6

PROBABLY NO MEAT IS MORE VERSATILE THAN LAMB. THIS NONTRADITIONAL CURRY BLENDS AROMATIC GROUND
SPICES WITH THE SWEETNESS OF ORANGE JUICE AND THE CLEANSING FRESHNESS OF GREEN CHILIES AND MINT.
IT IS A THICK, WET CURRY, IDEAL FOR SERVING WITH BREAD FOR MOPPING UP THE JUICES.

oil	3 tablespoons
onions	2, finely diced
garlic	4 cloves, crushed
ginger	3 teaspoons finely grated
ground cumin	2 teaspoons
ground coriander	2 teaspoons
ground turmeric	1/2 teaspoon
cayenne pepper	1/2 teaspoon
garam masala	1 teaspoon
ground lamb	2 pounds 4 ounces
plain yogurt	1/3 cup
orange juice	1 cup
orange zest	2 teaspoons
bay leaf	1
long green chili	1, seeded, thinly sliced
cilantro	1 handful leaves, roughly chopped
mint	1 handful, roughly chopped

Heat the oil in a large, heavy-based frying pan over medium heat. Add the onion, garlic, and ginger and sauté for 5 minutes. Add the cumin, coriander, turmeric, cayenne pepper, and garam masala, and cook for an additional 5 minutes.

Increase the heat to high, add the lamb, and stir constantly while cooking to break the meat up. Add the yogurt, a tablespoon at a time, stirring so that it combines well. Add the orange juice, zest, and bay leaf.

Bring to a boil, then reduce to a simmer, cover, and cook for 45 minutes or until tender. While cooking, skim and discard any oil that surfaces. Season well to taste, then stir in the chili, cilantro, and mint before serving.

Native to southern Europe and the Mediterranean, fresh cilantro and coriander seeds are, nevertheless, an essential element in curries. The leaves, stems, and roots from the plant can all be used. The roots are used in curry pastes and sauces, the stems are used when a strong flavor is needed, and the leaves are added at the end of cooking to flavor and garnish. Fresh cilantro is fragrant with a gingery edge, while the dried seeds have a sweeter, slightly peppery aroma. The flavor and aroma of the whole seeds are enhanced if they are lightly dry-fried before they are crushed.

three ways with bread

A CURRY SERVED ON ITS OWN IS NO CURRY AT ALL. RICE, SIDE DISHES OF RAITAS OR CHUTNEYS, AND BREADS SUCH AS NAAN ARE WHAT MAKES THEM COMPLETE. FURTHERMORE, IT'S A RARE CURRY THAT DOES NOT HAPPILY LEND ITSELF TO BEING SCOOPED UP WITH SOME BREAD. HERE ARE THREE CLASSIC CHOICES: DRY, UNLEAVENED ROTIS AND CHAPATIS, THE BASIC EVERYDAY BREADS OF INDIA; AND SOFT, OVEN-BAKED NAANS, WHICH ARE LEAVENED WITH A STARTER TO GIVE THEM THEIR PUFFED APPEARANCE.

roti

Sift 3 cups roti or all-purpose flour into a large mixing bowl with 1 teaspoon salt. Rub in 2 tablespoons softened ghee or oil with your fingertips. Add 1 lightly beaten egg and 1 cup warm water, and mix together with a flat-bladed knife to form a moist dough. Turn out onto a well-floured surface and knead for 10 minutes or until you have a soft dough. Sprinkle with more flour as necessary. Form the dough into a ball and brush with oil. Place in a bowl, cover, and let sit for 2 hours. On a lightly floured surface, divide the dough into twelve pieces and roll into even-size balls. Take one ball and, with a little oil on your fingertips, hold the ball in the air and work around the edge, pulling out the dough until a 1/16-inch thick, 6-inch round is formed. Lay on a lightly floured surface and cover with plastic wrap so it doesn't dry out. Repeat the process with the remaining balls. Heat a large frying pan over high heat and brush it with ghee or oil. Carefully place one roti in the frying pan, brush with some extra beaten egg, and cook for 1 minute or until the underside is golden. Slide onto a plate and brush the pan with some more ghee or oil. Cook the other side of the roti for 50–60 seconds or until golden. Remove from the pan and cover to keep warm. Cook the remaining rotis in the same way. Makes 12.

chapati

Put 2 1/4 cups atta (chapati) flour in a large bowl with a pinch of salt. Slowly add 1 cup water, or enough to form a firm dough. Knead on a lightly floured surface until smooth. Cover with plastic wrap and let sit for 50 minutes. Divide into fourteen portions and roll into 5 1/2-inch circles. Heat a frying pan over medium heat and brush with melted ghee or oil. Cook the chapatis one at a time, flattening their surfaces, for 2–3 minutes on each side or until bubbles appear and the chapatis are golden brown. Makes 14.

naan

Preheat the oven to 400°F. Lightly grease two 10 x 15-inch baking sheets. Sift together 4 cups all-purpose flour, 1 teaspoon baking powder, 1/2 teaspoon baking soda, and 1 teaspoon salt. Mix in 1 beaten egg, 1 tablespoon melted ghee or butter, and 1/2 cup plain yogurt, and gradually add enough milk to form a soft dough—about 1 cup. Cover with a damp cloth and let sit in a warm place for 2 hours. Knead the dough on a well-floured surface for 2–3 minutes or until smooth. Divide into eight portions and roll each one into an oval 6 inches long. Brush with water and place, wet side down, on the prepared baking sheets. Brush with melted ghee or butter and bake for 8–10 minutes or until golden brown. To make garlic naan, crush 6 garlic cloves and sprinkle evenly over the dough prior to baking. Makes 8.

snapper with green bananas and mango

. . . . serves 4

THIS IMPRESSIVE-LOOKING CURRY IS RICHLY FLAVORED WITH SPICES, HERBS, AND TROPICAL FRUIT. ROBUST FRUIT LIKE GREEN BANANAS MAKES AN INTERESTING TEXTURAL ADDITION TO CURRIES—THE BANANA IS VERY STARCHY, MORE LIKE A VEGETABLE THAN A FRUIT, AND WILL HELP TO THICKEN THE CURRY.

curry paste

coriander seeds	3 teaspoons
cumin seeds	1 teaspoon
dried long red chilies	2–3
lemongrass	2 stems, white part only, thinly sliced
red Asian shallots	3, finely chopped
garlic	2 cloves, crushed
ground turmeric	1 teaspoon
shrimp paste	1 teaspoon
ground turmeric	1 teaspoon
green banana (or plantain)	1 small, thinly sliced
unsweetened coconut cream	3 tablespoons
fish sauce	1 tablespoon
jaggery	1 teaspoon shaved (or 1 teaspoon brown sugar)
snapper or other skinless, firm white fish fillets	14 ounces, cut into large cubes
unsweetened coconut milk	1 1/4 cups
mango	1 small, just ripe, cut into thin slices
long green chili	1, thinly sliced
Thai basil leaves	12

Dry-fry the coriander and cumin seeds in a frying pan over medium-high heat for 2–3 minutes or until fragrant. Allow to cool. Using a mortar with a pestle or a spice grinder, crush or grind into a powder.

Soak the chilies in boiling water for 5 minutes or until soft. Remove the stem and seeds, then chop. Put the chilies and the ground coriander and cumin seeds with the remaining curry paste ingredients in a food processor or in a mortar with a pestle. Process or pound into a smooth paste. Add a little oil if it is too thick.

Bring a small saucepan of water to a boil. Add 1 teaspoon salt, turmeric, and banana. Simmer for 10 minutes, then drain.

Put the coconut cream in a large saucepan, bring to a rapid simmer over medium heat, stirring occasionally, and cook for 5–10 minutes or until the mixture "splits" (the oil starts to separate). Add 2 tablespoons of the curry paste, stir well to combine, and cook until fragrant. Add the fish sauce and jaggery, and cook for 2 minutes or until the mixture begins to darken. Stir the fish pieces well in the curry mixture to coat. Slowly add the coconut milk until it has all been incorporated.

Add the banana, mango, chili, and Thai basil to the pan, and gently stir all the ingredients. Cook for an additional 1–2 minutes, then serve.

minted lamb curry

WONDERFULLY FRESH TASTING, MINT IS MORE OFTEN ASSOCIATED WITH CHUTNEYS, SALADS, AND TEAS THAN CURRIES, BUT THIS SIMPLE DISH PROVES THAT IT CAN WORK WELL IN THIS ARENA, TOO. HERE, IT IS COMBINED WITH CILANTRO, GREEN CHILIES, AND LEMON JUICE TO CREATE A REFRESHING CURRY.

lamb shoulder	2 pounds 4 ounces, cut into 3/4-inch cubes
onions	4, thinly sliced
garlic	3 cloves, crushed
ginger	3 teaspoons finely chopped
cayenne pepper	1/2 teaspoon
ground turmeric	1 teaspoon
chicken stock	1/2 cup
cilantro	1 handful leaves and stalks
mint	1 handful
long green chilies	3
lemon juice	3 tablespoons
sugar	1 teaspoon

Put the lamb, onion, garlic, ginger, cayenne pepper, turmeric, and stock in a heavy-based saucepan over medium heat. Bring to a simmer, reduce the heat to low, then cover and cook for 2 hours. Skim and discard any oil that surfaces.

Put the cilantro leaves and stalks, mint leaves, chilies, lemon juice, and 2 tablespoons of cooking liquid from the curry in a food processor or in a mortar with a pestle. Process or pound into a smooth consistency. Pour into the lamb mixture, and put back on the heat until it just comes back up to a simmer. Add the sugar, season well to taste, and serve.

Throughout its culinary history, mint has been used with remarkable consistency—that is, with meat (particularly lamb), in drinks, and in sauces and pickles. In India and Southeast Asia, it appears in cold and hot drinks, salads, chutneys, raitas, and desserts—as well as in the occasional curry. In these countries, where much of the food is hot and spicy, mint is greatly valued for its cooling properties and sweet, light flavor. There are many local varieties of mint, but common garden mint is a fine substitute. Buy fresh leaves and store for up to a week in the refrigerator, or tightly seal in a bag and freeze.

vietnamese mild chicken curry .... serves 6

VIETNAMESE FOOD IS AN INTRIGUING MIX OF INDIGENOUS, FRENCH, AND ASIAN INFLUENCES. CURRIES ARE FOUND MAINLY IN THE TROPICAL SOUTHERN AREAS OF THE COUNTRY, AND THOUGH OFTEN SHOWING LINKS WITH INDIAN COOKING, ARE NOT AS RICH OR AS SPICY AS THOSE FROM INDIA OR THAILAND.

chicken leg quarters	4 large
Indian curry powder	1 tablespoon
superfine sugar	1 teaspoon
ground black pepper	1/2 teaspoon
oil	1/3 cup
orange sweet potato	1 large (about 1 pound 2 ounces), cut into 1 1/4-inch cubes
onion	1 large, cut into thin wedges
garlic	4 cloves, crushed
lemongrass	1 stem, white part only, finely chopped
bay leaves	2
carrot	1 large, cut into 1/2-inch pieces diagonally
unsweetened coconut milk	14 fluid-ounce can, or 1 2/3 cups
Thai basil leaves	to serve

Remove the skin and any excess fat from the chicken. Pat dry with paper towels and cut each quarter into three even pieces. Put the curry powder, sugar, pepper, and 2 teaspoons salt in a bowl. Mix well. Rub the curry mixture into the chicken pieces. Put the chicken pieces on a plate, cover with plastic wrap, and refrigerate overnight.

Heat the oil in a large saucepan over medium heat. Add the sweet potato and cook for 3 minutes or until lightly golden. Remove with a slotted spoon.

Remove all but 2 tablespoons of the oil from the pan. Add the onion and cook, stirring, for 5 minutes. Add the garlic, lemongrass, and bay leaves, and cook for 2 minutes.

Add the chicken and cook, stirring, over medium heat for 5 minutes or until well coated in the mixture and starting to brown. Add 1 cup water and simmer covered, stirring occasionally, for 20 minutes.

Stir in the sweet potato, carrot, and coconut milk. Simmer uncovered, stirring occasionally, for 30 minutes or until the chicken is cooked and tender. Be careful not to break up the sweet potato cubes. Serve garnished with basil leaves.

Remove the skin and any excess fat from the chicken.

Sauté the sweet potato until lightly golden.

Pour in the coconut milk and simmer until the chicken is tender.

thai sweet pork and pineapple curry

THIS REFRESHING CURRY IS A VIBRANT MIX OF FRESH INGREDIENTS—PINEAPPLE, TOMATOES, CUCUMBER, AND CILANTRO—AND SWEET–SOUR SEASONINGS SUCH AS VINEGAR AND JAGGERY. THIS COMBINATION MAKES IT A GREAT SUMMER DISH: IT HAS A REFRESHING, SLIGHTLY SPICY AND SWEET FLAVOR.

boneless pork leg	1 pound 2 ounces, trimmed of excess fat
oil	1 tablespoon
garlic	3 cloves, crushed
brown malt vinegar	1/2 cup
jaggery	1/4 cup shaved (or 1/4 cup brown sugar)
tomato paste	3 tablespoons
tomato	1, cut into wedges
onion	1, cut into thin wedges
pineapple	1/2 cup cut into chunks
English cucumber	1/2, halved lengthwise, seeded, sliced
red bell pepper	1/2, cut into strips
jalapeño chilies	2 1/2 tablespoons in brine, chopped
scallions	2, cut into 2-inch pieces
cilantro	1 small handful leaves

Cut the pork into 1 1/4-inch cubes. Heat the oil in a large saucepan over medium heat. Add the pork and garlic, and cook for 4–5 minutes or until the pork is lightly browned.

In another saucepan, stir the vinegar, jaggery, tomato paste, and 1/2 teaspoon salt over medium heat for 3 minutes or until the jaggery dissolves.

Add the vinegar mixture to the pork along with the tomato, onion, pineapple, cucumber, bell pepper, and chilies. Bring to a boil, then reduce to a simmer and cook for 8–10 minutes or until the pork is tender. Stir in the scallion and cilantro leaves and serve.

Trim the pork of excess fat and cut into neat cubes.

Add the cucumber and red bell pepper to the saucepan.

the perfect spice blend

A spice blend is a wonderful synergy of complementary spices. Whole spices—being the dried seeds, stems, bark, or roots of particular plants—are dry-fried or roasted, then finely ground to a powder to release their natural, aromatic oils. The most commonly known of these spice blends is curry powder. This mixture comes in several guises, forming the flavor structure for many curries, particularly Indian and Sri Lankan varieties. Although mainly used as the base flavor for cooked dishes, some spice blends, such as garam masala or five-spice, are often utilized at the end of the cooking process as a final aromatic addition to a dish.

For convenience, you will find most well-known spice blends in supermarkets and Asian food stores but, as with curry pastes, fresh is undoubtedly best. Fresh, whole spices retain many of the natural oils, which carry flavor and aroma. If the spices are old or have been preground for some time, they may have lost flavor due to age and exposure to air. So it is best to buy small amounts of whole spices and replace them as required.

To make your own spice blend, first dry-fry the spices in a frying pan over medium-high heat for 2–3 minutes or until fragrant. Ideally, dry-fry each spice separately to obtain optimum flavor, as certain spices, depending on size and moisture content, will take longer than others to become fragrant. This process mellows the flavor of the spices, making for a well-rounded final result in your cooking. Allow the spices to cool, then put them in a mortar and pound with a pestle until finely ground. You can also use a coffee or spice grinder. Store ground spices in a clean, well-sealed glass jar for up to three weeks, at which time the flavor will diminish rapidly.

lamb rizala
.... serves 6

THIS RECIPE IS A STUDY IN HOW TO PRODUCE MELT-IN-THE-MOUTH TENDER, FLAVORSOME MEAT. TRADITIONALLY, RIZALA FEATURED MUTTON, SO SLOW, GENTLE COOKING WAS THE IDEAL METHOD, BUT THIS APPLIES EQUALLY TO LAMB SHOULDER. THE YOGURT FURTHER TENDERIZES THE MEAT, HELPING IT ABSORB THE AROMATICS.

onions	2, chopped
ginger	1 tablespoon grated
garlic	4 cloves, crushed
ground cinnamon	1 teaspoon
ghee or oil	3 tablespoons
lamb shoulder	2 pounds 4 ounces, diced
plain yogurt	½ cup
chicken stock	1 cup
crisp fried onions	½ cup
red chilies	3, seeded, thinly sliced
sugar	1 tablespoon
lime juice	3 tablespoons

Put the onion, ginger, garlic, cinnamon, and 3 tablespoons water in a food processor or in a mortar with a pestle, and process or pound into a smooth paste.

Heat the ghee or oil in a heavy-based saucepan over high heat. Brown the lamb in batches and set aside.

Reduce the heat to low, add the onion paste, and cook for 5 minutes, stirring constantly. Put the lamb back into the pan, and stir to combine. Then add the yogurt a spoonful at a time, stirring well to incorporate. Add the stock and crisp fried onions. Bring to a simmer, cover, and cook over low heat for 2 hours. While cooking, skim and discard any oil that surfaces.

When the lamb is tender, add the chilies, sugar, and lime juice, and cook for another 5 minutes before serving.

Garlic is a bedrock of most cuisines, and it is no different for the cuisines of India and Southeast Asia. In these regions, it is used in relishes and chutneys, vegetable dishes, stir-fries, roasted meats, breads, pickles and, of course, curries. Unmistakably pungent, its taste can vary from biting to mellow, depending on how it is prepared. Of the many varieties of this hardy, bulbous herb, each differs in size, pungency, and color— Asian garlic is generally much smaller than Western varieties. Garlic is freshest in the summer when the bulbs are firm. Choose fresh, plump-looking bulbs with a white skin and store in a cool, open place.

chicken curry with apricots . . . . serves 6–8

THIS DISH IS A LOVELY BLEND OF SWEET, RICH APRICOTS AND MELLOW, ROUND SPICES SUCH AS CUMIN, TURMERIC, AND CARDAMOM. WITH FRESH GINGER AND GREEN CHILIES PROVIDING A BIT OF BITE, THE CHICKEN ITSELF SEEMS LIKE AN ALMOST INCIDENTAL INGREDIENT!

dried apricots	18
ghee or oil	1 tablespoon
chickens	two 3-pound 5-ounce, jointed
onions	3, thinly sliced
ginger	1 teaspoon grated
garlic	3 cloves, crushed
long green chilies	3, seeded, finely chopped
cumin seeds	1 teaspoon
chili powder	1 teaspoon
ground turmeric	1/2 teaspoon
cardamom pods	4, bruised
tomatoes	4 large, peeled, cut into eight pieces

Soak the dried apricots in 1 cup hot water for 1 hour.

Heat the ghee or oil in a large saucepan, add the chicken in batches, and cook over high heat for 5–6 minutes or until browned. Remove from the pan. Add the onion and cook, stirring often, for 10 minutes or until the onion has softened and turned golden brown.

Add the ginger, garlic, and chilies. Stirring, cook for 2 minutes. Stir in the cumin seeds, chili powder, and turmeric, and cook for an additional 1 minute.

Return the chicken to the pan, add the cardamom, tomatoes, and apricots, with any remaining soaking liquid, and mix well. Simmer covered for 35 minutes or until the chicken is tender.

Remove the chicken, cover, and keep warm. Bring the liquid to a boil and boil rapidly uncovered for 5 minutes or until it thickens slightly. To serve, spoon the liquid over the chicken.

Sauté the chicken pieces in batches until browned.

Stir the spices into the onion mixture and cook until fragrant.

Add the chicken, cardamom, tomatoes, and apricots to the pan.

thai beef and butternut squash curry............serves 6

CURRIES ARE AS MUCH ABOUT AROMA AS THEY ARE ABOUT TASTE, BUT THIS CURRY ALSO CONTRIBUTES A WONDERFUL TENDER TEXTURE TO THE MIX. SOFT, SWEET WINTER SQUASH; MOIST, RICH BEEF; AND CRUNCHY PEANUTS COME TOGETHER IN A SAUCE THAT IS HOT, RICH, AND SWEET.

oil	2 tablespoons
blade steak	1 pound 10 ounces, thinly sliced
musaman curry paste	4 tablespoons, store-bought or see recipe on page 17
garlic	2 cloves, crushed
onion	1, sliced
curry leaves	6, torn, plus extra leaves for garnish
unsweetened coconut milk	3 cups
butternut squash	3 cups roughly diced
raw peanuts	2 tablespoons, chopped
jaggery	1 tablespoon shaved (or 1 tablespoon brown sugar)
tamarind puree	2 tablespoons
fish sauce	2 tablespoons

Heat a wok or frying pan over high heat. Add the oil and swirl to coat the side. Add the meat in batches and cook for 5 minutes or until browned. Remove the meat from the wok.

Add the curry paste, garlic, onion, and curry leaves to the wok, and stir to coat. Return the meat to the wok and cook, stirring, over medium heat for 2 minutes.

Add the coconut milk to the wok, then reduce the heat and simmer for 45 minutes. Add the butternut squash and simmer for 25–30 minutes or until the meat and the squash are tender and the sauce thickens.

Stir in the peanuts, jaggery, tamarind, and fish sauce, and simmer for 1 minute. Garnish with the extra curry leaves and serve.

Pour the coconut milk into the curry mixture and simmer.

Add the squash and simmer until tender and the sauce thickens.

chiang mai pork curry

THIS BURMESE-STYLE CURRY IS TYPICAL OF THE CHIANG MAI AREA IN THAILAND'S NORTH. IT IS UNLIKE THE MAJORITY OF FRAGRANT THAI CURRIES IN THAT IT HAS A SPICIER, ALMOST INDIAN FLAVOR. GENERALLY MADE WITH PORK, YOU WILL OCCASIONALLY FIND IT MADE WITH CHICKEN. THIS CURRY IMPROVES IF MADE IN ADVANCE.

chiang mai curry paste

coriander seeds	1 tablespoon
cumin seeds	2 teaspoons
dried long red chilies	2
salt	1/2 teaspoon
galangal	2-inch piece, grated
lemongrass	1 stem, white part only, finely chopped
red Asian shallots	2, chopped
garlic cloves	2, crushed
ground turmeric	1/4 teaspoon
shrimp paste	1 teaspoon
ground cinnamon	1/2 teaspoon
pork belly	1 pound 2 ounces, cut into cubes
oil	2 tablespoons
garlic	2 cloves, crushed
red Asian shallots	4, crushed with the blade of a cleaver
ginger	3 teaspoons grated
unsalted roasted peanuts	4 tablespoons
tamarind puree	3 tablespoons
fish sauce	2 tablespoons
jaggery	2 tablespoons shaved (or 2 tablespoons brown sugar)

Dry-fry the coriander and cumin seeds in a frying pan over medium-high heat for 2–3 minutes or until fragrant. Allow to cool. Using a mortar with a pestle or a spice grinder, crush or grind into a powder.

Soak the chilies in boiling water for 5 minutes or until soft. Remove the stem and seeds, then chop. Put the chilies and the ground coriander and cumin seeds with the remaining curry paste ingredients in a food processor or in a mortar with a pestle. Process or pound into a smooth paste. Add a little oil if it is too thick.

Blanch the pork cubes in boiling water for 1 minute, then drain well. Heat the oil in a wok or saucepan and fry the garlic for 1 minute. Add 2 tablespoons of the curry paste and stir-fry until fragrant. Add the pork, shallots, ginger, and peanuts. Stir briefly. Add 2 cups water and the tamarind and bring to a boil.

Add the fish sauce and jaggery, and simmer for 1 1/4 hours or until the pork is very tender. Add more water as the pork cooks, if necessary.

index

Thunder Bay Press
An imprint of the Advantage Publishers Group
5880 Oberlin Drive, San Diego, CA 92121-4794
www.thunderbaybooks.com

All notations of errors or omissions should be addressed to Thunder Bay Press, Editorial Department, at the above address. All other correspondence (author inquiries, permissions) concerning the content of this book should be addressed to Murdoch Books Pty Limited, Pier 8/9 23 Hickson Road, Millers Point NSW 2000 Australia.

ISBN-13: 978-1-59223-534-6
ISBN-10: 1-59223-534-4
Library of Congress Cataloging-in-Publication Data available upon request.

Printed by Toppan Printing Hong Kong Co. Ltd. Printed in China.
1 2 3 4 5   09 08 07 06 05

IMPORTANT: Those who might be at risk from the effects of salmonella poisoning (the elderly, pregnant women, young children, and those suffering from immune deficiency diseases) should consult their doctor with any concerns about eating raw eggs.

CONVERSION GUIDE: You may find cooking times vary depending on the oven you are using. For convection ovens, as a general rule, set the oven temperature to 70°F lower than indicated in the recipe.

Chief Executive: Juliet Rogers
Publisher: Kay Scarlett
Design concept and art direction: Vivien Valk
Designer: Heather Menzies
Project manager and editor: Paul McNally
Text: Margaret Malone
Food editor: Jane Lawson
Recipes: Vanessa Broadfood, Vicky Harris and the Murdoch Books Test Kitchen
Photographer: Ashley Mackevicius
Stylist: Wendy Berecry
Food preparation: Ross Dobson and Abi Ulgiati
Production: Adele Troeger